PRAISE FOR MELODY WILDING, LMSW, AND *TRUST YOURSELF*

T0023260

"Invaluable lessons on overcoming imposter sy
communication to increase your confidence. If
or overshadowed by the world's harsher or mor
this awesomely helpful book—and you'll never a₅   ......pret 'You're too sensitive' as an insult."

—APPLE BOOKS (Best Books of May 2021)

"Wilding has an important message for high-performing professionals who happen to be highly attuned with their feelings: Don't let your emotions get in the
way of your success."

—*TD* MAGAZINE

"*Trust Yourself* is both an empathetic exploration of the power of sensitivity, specifically in high achievers, and an actionable guide to mastering it."

—MCKINSEY COMPANY

"From chapters covering stress to perfectionism and self-doubt to imposter syndrome, Melody Wilding's powerful book is here to help relieve us from the
burdens that hold us back from achieving success at work. In *Trust Yourself*,
you build the tools to achieve confidence, find your voice, build resilience, and
enjoy your success all while staying true to who you are."

—POPSUGAR

"Groundbreaking and insightful, *Trust Yourself* is essential reading for every sensitive, introverted professional. Wilding does a brilliant job of giving you tools
to regain your confidence and become your most empowered self."

—SUSAN CAIN, author of *Quiet* and creator of Quiet Revolution

"In a world that constantly urges us to *be* more and *do* more, many of us wind up
feeling never good enough or smart enough. *Trust Yourself* takes you on a gentle
journey of self-discovery and provides the encouragement and tools needed to
get out of the rat race and back into the human race. Wilding's is the voice we
all need inside of our heads guiding us to make healthier choices for a more
fulfilling life."

—LOIS P. FRANKEL, PhD, author of *Nice Girls Don't Get the Corner Office*

"Every organization, whether aware of it or not, needs highly sensitive people. Some of them, the 'Sensitive Strivers,' really belong in an organization. At the top! Or running their own. *Trust Yourself* is an exquisite road map written just for Sensitive Strivers looking to thrive in the workplace."

—**DR. ELAINE ARON**, bestselling author of *The Highly Sensitive Person*

"*Trust Yourself* is a practical, empathetic, and refreshingly relatable guide to setting—and honoring—the boundaries you need to achieve personal and professional fulfillment. A must-read for anyone seeking a life with less stress and more success."

—**LIZ FOSSLIEN**, coauthor and illustrator of *No Hard Feelings*

"Wilding's message—trust yourself—is much needed."

—**JULIA CAMERON**, author of *The Artist's Way*

"You could burn out trying to succeed, or you could read this book. The engaging strategies, practical tips, and exercises in *Trust Yourself* will help any Sensitive Striver excel at work and level up in their career."

—**ALEXANDRA CAVOULACOS**, founder of The Muse

"Larger-than-life expectations have led to more pressure at work and a surge in imposter syndrome. In *Trust Yourself*, Melody Wilding leads with empathy and delivers foolproof strategies that anyone can use to overcome doubt and reclaim their confidence."

—**GEORGENE HUANG**, CEO and cofounder of Fairygodboss

"I found myself nodding my head a lot while reading this book. *Trust Yourself* helps us gain self-awareness around the qualities that make us Sensitive Strivers and gives us the tools to assess how these individual qualities serve us or deplete us so we can direct our energy towards becoming the person we aspire to be."

—**FRAN HAUSER**, startup investor and author of *The Myth of the Nice Girl*

"Working with Melody gave me the courage to channel my sensitivity into a super strength. I will be giving everyone on my team this book. *Trust Yourself* is a must-read for every heart-centered, empathetic leader and professional who wants success without so much stress."

—**CLAUDE SILVER**, Chief Heart Officer, VaynerMedia

Trust Yourself

TRUST YOURSELF

Stop Overthinking and Channel Your Emotions for Success at Work

MELODY J. WILDING, LMSW

CHRONICLE PRISM

First Chronicle Books LLC paperback edition, published in 2022.
Originally published in hardcover in 2021 by Chronicle Books LLC.

Library of Congress Cataloging-in-Publication Data

Names: Wilding, Melody J., author.
Title: Trust yourself : stop overthinking and channel your emotions for
success at work / Melody J. Wilding, LMSW.
Description: San Francisco, California : Chronicle Prism, [2021] |
Includes bibliographical references. | Identifiers:
LCCN 2020043646 | ISBN 9781797201962 (hardcover) |
ISBN 9781797202006 (paperback) | ISBN 9781797201993 (ebook)
Subjects: LCSH: Women—Vocational guidance. | Confidence. |
Self-esteem in women. | Self-realization in women. | Success in business.
Classification: LCC HF5382.6 .W554 2021 | DDC 650.1082—dc23
LC record available at https://lccn.loc.gov/2020043646

Manufactured in the United States of America.

Cover design by Kathleen Lynch/Black Kat Design.
Book design by Pamela Geismar.
Typesetting by Maureen Forys, Happenstance Type-O-Rama. Typeset in
Cormorant Garamond, Trade Gothic, Franklin Gothic, and Manus.

Names in this book have been changed to ensure privacy and confidentiality.

10 9 8 7 6 5 4 3 2 1

Chronicle books and gifts are available at special quantity discounts
to corporations, professional associations, literacy programs, and other
organizations. For details and discount information, please contact
our premiums department at corporatesales@chroniclebooks.com or at
1-800-759-0190.

CHRONICLE PRISM

Chronicle Prism is an imprint of Chronicle Books LLC,
680 Second Street, San Francisco, California 94107

www.chronicleprism.com

*For Mom and Dad, who believed in me
even when I didn't believe in myself.
I love you with all my heart.*

INTRODUCTION

*"Can you remember who you were, before the
world told you who you should be?"*

—CHARLES BUKOWSKI

IT HIT ME LIKE A TON OF BRICKS one Saturday night. Sitting at a half-empty
Starbucks on the Upper East Side, I realized I had made a *terrible* mistake.

For months, I had looked forward to a close friend's wedding weekend. My hotel was paid for. Travel arrangements had been made. I couldn't
wait to celebrate the bride and to see all of my college friends in one
place. But, in the week leading up to the wedding, new projects piled up
at work, and I felt enormous pressure—both internal and external—to be
available and responsive 24/7. I couldn't stop obsessing about my never-
ending to-do list, I found myself feeling guilty about taking time off, and
I agonized about whether or not I should actually go. One part of me
craved time away filled with fun, laughter, and relaxation while another
reminded me how behind I felt and how much I could get done if I stayed
home. At the last minute, I bailed. Sure, I was making the right decision
for my career, but that Saturday, while my friends celebrated together, I
was alone with my laptop, swimming in regret.

All my life, I had been a classic A-plus, gold-star, *good girl* who lived to exceed expectations. Diligent and disciplined, I worked hard to earn high grades in school, graduated at the top of my college class while balancing multiple jobs, and went on to get a master's in social work from Columbia University, so I could work in mental health. I dreamed of becoming a therapist, until well-meaning loved ones and advisors cautioned against it. *You can't make money as a therapist. You should go into healthcare or technology—something more stable and lucrative.* I followed their advice and took a job as a researcher at a fast-paced healthcare center in Manhattan.

From the outside, it looked like I had it all. I was accomplished, lived in a big city, and had a clear career path. But on the inside, I was frazzled, restless, and depleted. Rather than seeing my psychological state for what it was—a sign that my habits and behaviors were unsustainable—I took my sadness and disappointment to heart. Everyone else seemed so together. What was wrong with me?

Though I had no way of knowing it then, I wasn't alone when it came to how I felt. Sensitive, ambitious people are often so worried about what others think and so influenced by common definitions of success that they don't know how to direct their energy toward what they really want—a fulfilling life coupled with a sense of confidence and control. They've been taught that *achievement* means climbing to the top of the career ladder, but even when they do, they often feel empty, or experience relentless pressure to accomplish even *more*. And when this leads to burnout, these individuals assume the problem lies with them, instead of considering that, perhaps, they need to approach their careers (and their relationships with themselves) in a new way.

Looking back, my decision to skip the wedding made zero sense, but in retrospect I'm glad I made that terrible choice. That summer night forced me to step back and take a hard look at the feelings, thoughts, and behaviors that had brought me to this point. In addition to my research job, I had slowly been building a coaching practice during the previous three years based on my training in psychology; now I had no choice but to use the tools I had used with my clients on myself. When I began to unravel my self-sabotaging habits, I realized that the crux of the problem went deeper than just managing my time and the logistics of my full-time job and the business I was trying to build. The issue was an internal one: I had ignored my well-being and personal goals in favor of pursuing what I assumed I *should* be doing without ever pausing to consider if it would *actually* be fulfilling to me.

It took years of work for me to gradually free up the mental and emotional bandwidth to admit that my job wasn't aligned with what I needed and wanted as a hardworking but also naturally sensitive person. More importantly, through my coaching work, I discovered many sensitive high achievers like me who were struggling with problems like overthinking, emotional reactivity, perfectionism, and poor boundaries. Over time, I realized I wanted to help this particular group, who I call Sensitive Strivers, harness the power of their built-in sensitivities, which eventually led to me leaving my career in healthcare and expanding my coaching practice.

Trust Yourself is the book I wish I'd had as an empathetic, driven person trying to find my way in my career *and* figure out how to believe in myself in the process. This book is a guide to master your sensitivity and enjoy success—however you define it—without stress and overwhelm. Instead of feeling ordered around by your anxieties or your own unrealistically high expectations, you can feel in charge of your own life. And once you redirect your sensitive striving toward strength and not self-sabotage, you can move through the world with ease and reach your full potential.

Drawing on my experiences as a coach and professor of human behavior, this book combines stories based on my clients' experiences with sound, actionable tools you can use to cut through the stress, identify your purpose, and find the confidence to be true to who you are. Together with new insights, you'll walk away from each chapter with action items to work on and strategies to navigate the changes you're about to make. It's entirely possible to channel your ambition in healthy ways and to use your sensitivity as the superpower that it is—and this book will show you how.

Why You Picked Up This Book

You might be burned out like I was and facing down the realization that your work habits aren't sustainable. You may have recently been promoted, landed a new job, or have another opportunity that's leading you to think, *This is my moment!* Naturally, you want to bring your best to the situation—to get to the next level career-wise *and* to continue growing as a human being. You may be excited but worried about your ability to handle the workload and pressure. Or maybe you're facing factors outside your control or overall uncertainty in your career and, as a Sensitive Striver, you want to get better at rebounding from setbacks when and if they come.

Whatever the circumstance, you likely want how you feel on the *inside* to match the image of success you portray on the *outside*. Because most of all, you're probably sick and tired of getting in your own way. You want to understand and move past your insecurities so that you can . . .

- Drop the mental gymnastics of self-doubt, worry, and fear that limit your potential
- Enjoy your success without sacrificing your well-being or what's most important to you
- Feel secure in your judgment without a sneaking sense of doubt

I'm also willing to bet that you picked up this book looking for hope—hope that you can change, hope that you can develop steadfast belief in yourself that isn't contingent on how productive you are, hope that you're not crazy for being so affected by everything around you. Let me assure you that you are not alone. There are thousands, if not millions, of other sensitive, driven women and men out there who have wrestled with inadequacy and are thriving because they've learned how to channel their qualities in constructive ways.

The Path to Personal and Professional Fulfillment

The tools in this book are backed by decades of research and proven to work by my coaching clients. You may recognize some of these concepts from psychology, including cognitive-behavioral and mindfulness methods. I also infuse behavior change and neuroscience with communication, leadership, and career development skills.

I won't ask you to spend hours reflecting on your childhood; I won't have you complete a personal vision statement that makes you want to gag. Instead, you'll be prompted to take concrete steps that will change your habits and behavior for the better, starting *today*.

The typical order of operations on the road to finding personal and professional fulfillment is to:

1. *Reflect on who you are and who you want to become*

2. *Define your purpose and what you want for your life and career*

3. *Change your day-to-day actions*

But in my experience, stress makes it impossible for many sensitive, ambitious individuals to wrap their heads around the *big picture*, and they struggle to define what they actually want because they've spent so many years accommodating the demands of others.

That's why this book turns the conventional approach on its head.

- In Part I, you'll build self-awareness, so you can understand how your sensitivity has shaped your behavior as well as your view of yourself and your career.

- In Part II, you'll begin to tame self-sabotage (from overthinking and emotional reactivity to people-pleasing), so you can put in place healthier habits to support your sensitivity instead of letting it drive you crazy.

- In Part III, you'll zoom out to uncover what you really want out of life (not what you think others expect of you), so you can reach personally meaningful goals. By aligning your ambition with your core values and desires, you'll achieve self-confidence and become the person you aspire to be.

- In Part IV, you'll learn how to make your changes last and sustain self-growth by overcoming obstacles and more assertively advocating for yourself.

That's right. We're not going to dive right into talking about your long-term plan. Instead, we'll start by directing your energy toward what should be your top priority—getting your day-to-day stress under control. The skills in this book layer on top of one another to help you first develop self-acceptance and emotional stability. From that foundation, you can look toward the future with a clear head.

What to Expect in This Book

In each chapter, there are three types of tools you'll encounter:

Strategies. High-level action plans you can test out when appropriate.

Get Unstuck tips. If the Strategy seems difficult at first, use these tips to get going.

Exercises. Step-by-step worksheets, fillables, and quizzes to record your progress, spark breakthroughs, and implement the strategies you'll learn. These are more time-intensive and best done when you can sit and work through them, like before or after work or on weekends.

Throughout the book, you'll also find **Speak Up Shortcuts**, which give you easy hacks to find your voice and stand up for yourself. You can find a library of printable templates and digital versions of the Exercises plus additional tools, articles, and resources at melodywilding.com/bonus.

THE FOUNDATION FOR YOUR TRANSFORMATION

There are four core values to trusting yourself that weave through everything in this book and light a path toward braver action.

1. INTENTIONALITY. Sensitive people are more deliberate and purposeful. You'll leverage those strengths throughout this book to proactively engage with and take control of how you relate to yourself and your work. You'll make conscious choices about how you speak to yourself, respond to situations, and make decisions about your future.

2. INTEGRITY. Integrity involves being true to who you are beyond rules, expectations, and messages from other people. It may mean eliciting side-eye when you do what's right for you, even if it's not what others agree with, understand, or approve of. As you enter this journey, commit to keep the promises you make to yourself. Throughout this book, you'll also need to call upon integrity to be honest with yourself, even when the truth is uncomfortable.

3. AGENCY. When you have a strong sense of personal agency, you're able to differentiate between real versus perceived limitations so you can reach your goals. Agency allows you to break free from self-defeating fears that hold you back from reaching what you're truly capable of. It's about taking ownership of your thoughts, feelings, and actions—and deeply knowing *you* control your happiness.

4. EASE. Right now, you probably struggle to relax. You likely can't remember the last time you did something just for the fun of it. Every setback may feel like the end of the world. Life and work just feel difficult all the time. If this rings true, then it's time to incorporate ease back into your life. Ease may not always equal easiness because trusting yourself is hard work! But try to bring a spirit of lightheartedness, curiosity, experimentation, and open-mindedness to this book.

As you begin this journey, think about what habits or patterns you want to change. The more specific, the better. Your personal results will depend in part on how much of yourself you bring to the process and how much work you're willing to put in. Keep in mind that at times you may feel like you're taking three steps forward and two steps back. You may doubt yourself, feel paralyzed by fear, or wonder why you started. When this happens, know that you're doing something right. It's simply your body and mind's way of trying to keep you safe and protected. Recognize those reactions, honor them, and understand that they serve a purpose (because all growth requires friction).

You'll get the most out of this book if you implement the Strategies and complete the Exercises, whether you work through them sequentially or skip around based on what you need the most. I recommend earmarking a special notebook to keep close to you and use as a safe, private space to do each one and also to capture your insights and action items in the moment. Writing these items down will help commit them to memory and will create a reference document, whether you need it tomorrow or a year from now. It also signals to your brain that this process is a priority, which will maximize your results.

When you're ready to work on the Exercises, find some time and space where you can concentrate and think clearly. Above all else, be patient with yourself and keep in mind that incremental, implementable, imperfect changes over time add up to big results. Remember, you have picked up this book to work on the most important thing in your life, *you*.

I'm here for you. I believe in you. Now, let's get started.

PART I

BUILD SELF-AWARENESS

1

Are You a Sensitive Striver?

2

Overcome the Honor Roll Hangover

3

Give Yourself Permission

ARE YOU A SENSITIVE STRIVER?

1

"I understand now that I'm not a mess, but a deeply feeling person in a messy world. I explain that now, when someone asks me why I cry so often: 'For the same reason I laugh so often— because I'm paying attention.'"

—GLENNON DOYLE

KELLY'S JOB WAS KILLING HER SPIRIT.

When she'd originally started as the Social Services Director at a large county agency six years before, she'd been excited to lead a team and to make a difference in the lives of underprivileged children. All her mentors said that with her drive, she was perfectly positioned to step into a VP role, and within three years, she had been promoted to Vice President of Programs, Operations, and Administration.

During the first year in the role, her new responsibilities were demanding yet manageable, but Kelly's team ended up short-staffed during her second year on the executive team. At first, Kelly didn't mind. She loved her job and took pride in being the go-to person at the agency. Besides, she had been taught that good employees always go above and beyond, and that's what she assumed she needed to do to continue advancing in her career.

As time went on, sixty-plus-hour weeks became Kelly's new normal. She filled in at board meetings and made decisions on behalf of her boss, who was an absentee manager. She picked up the slack no matter what. What finally pushed her over the edge was that in addition to her official job responsibilities, she was assigned to support a major project under the Executive Director. The demands had finally become too much, and Kelly reached a breaking point. Her hair began to fall out. She battled migraines. Work also affected her home life. Kelly was always glued to her phone and answering emails, including during family dinners. Her husband remarked that she had turned into a zombie. Her daughter complained that she missed *the old mom*.

As the months wore on, Kelly's colleagues told her almost daily that the agency would collapse without her. She took their comments as a compliment, but the idea that she was indispensable kept her from being able to say no or to delegate. The thought of admitting to her boss that she couldn't handle so much made her impossibly anxious. What if he questioned her commitment? What if he fired her? Kelly told herself to work harder—that she was making a big deal out of nothing. The fact that the stress was now causing her to miss deadlines and to make mistakes on basic tasks only reinforced her belief that speaking up would jeopardize her image and her chances to further advance.

Kelly's wake-up call arrived when she was forced to take an eight-week medical leave after being hospitalized with shortness of breath and chest pain. She thought the time off would be enough, but from the moment she stepped foot back in the office, she felt a sense of dread. When the same anxiety and overworking crept up on her again, she finally decided to seek help. That's when she reached out to me about becoming her coach.

Kelly felt like she wasn't in control of her own life anymore. Every day was one long game of Whac-A-Mole, and she was so overwhelmed that she didn't (or couldn't) deal with issues until they became so serious they were impossible to ignore. She desperately wanted to feel more like herself again and to rediscover the fulfillment she once felt in her career. At the same time, fear and a preoccupation of what success should look like kept her sacrificing herself to measure up.

Though Kelly's case is extreme, many of my coaching clients come to me with tales like hers—of trading their well-being for the sake of getting ahead or getting the job done. They know something is *off*, but they don't know how to change things, and they're not quite sure what it will mean to give up long-standing thoughts, habits, and behaviors. Instead, they continue to live with their inner lives on overdrive, professionally successful, yes, but also highly influenced by their emotions and any feedback or criticism of their work. For Kelly and others, a moment of realization is the first step toward a breakthrough, both professionally and personally. I call Kelly and those like her *Sensitive Strivers*.

What Is a Sensitive Striver?

Sensitive Strivers are high achievers who are also more attuned to their emotions, the world, and the behavior of those around them. Many are former star students who bring that same dedication, reliability, and ambition into the workplace. But while many Sensitive Strivers rise quickly in their careers, they often face a daily battle with stress, anxiety, and self-doubt.

If all of this resonates with you, then welcome. You're in exactly the right place. This mix of qualities makes you who you are, and likely has made you super successful. On the one hand, people appreciate your warmth, depth of personality, and overall conscientiousness. On the other hand, situations that others find relatively easy, such as making decisions and recovering from setbacks, can send you into a downward spiral. As a Sensitive Striver, you may sometimes feel demoralized by the high expectations you place on yourself, which can lead to overthinking minor situations. You may also be prone to emotional overwhelm that shows up in the form of tears, panic, or complete withdrawal. That's because when sensitivity and achievement meet, it can be a tricky combination. Recently on Instagram, one of my followers summed up what it's like by saying, "I overeverything."

What Being a Sensitive Striver Is *Not*

You may be thinking to yourself that sensitive striving is just another form of being a perfectionist, an overachiever, or an introvert. While being a Sensitive Striver may overlap with one or more of the other categories, none of them adequately captures the struggles Sensitive Strivers face.

For instance:

- **Not all sensitive people are introverted.** Sensitive people and introverts share many qualities, such as a need for more downtime, but research shows that about 30 percent of sensitive people are extroverted, meaning they gain energy by being around people. Many introverts also do not consider a strong work ethic as a core part of their identities like Sensitive Strivers do.

- **Not all perfectionists are self-aware or accomplished in their careers.** In fact, the most successful people are rarely perfectionists (defined as a striving for flawlessness and setting high performance standards) because perfectionism cripples progress and leads to decision paralysis.

- **Not all overachievers are sensitive.** You can be an overachiever (defined as someone who performs better or achieves more success than expected) without experiencing the higher-than-normal reactivity that comes with being sensitive. Not all high performers experience challenges when encountering conflict, setting boundaries, or quieting negative thoughts like Sensitive Strivers do.

SO, ARE YOU A SENSITIVE STRIVER?

Check off the sentences that sound like you:

○ I experience emotions at a high level of depth and complexity.

○ I have a strong desire to exceed expectations in every aspect of my life.

○ I consider myself to be driven and enjoy pushing myself to achieve goals.

○ I crave meaning and fulfillment.

○ I need time to think through decisions before I act.

○ I have an inner critic that never takes a day off.

○ I'm kind, compassionate, and empathetic to others.

○ I have a keen ability to sense other people's feelings.

○ I tend to put other people's needs ahead of my own.

○ I find it difficult to set boundaries and often say yes too much.

○ I've struggled with burnout.

○ I'm easily impacted by stress.

○ I struggle to turn off my mind because it's constantly filled with thoughts.

○ I have strong emotional reactions.

○ I feel anxious when I'm caught off guard or know I'm being watched or evaluated.

○ I hold myself to high standards.

○ I try to get things right and judge myself harshly if I make mistakes.

○ I often get stuck in indecision and analysis paralysis.

○ I take feedback and criticism to heart.

If you checked off nine or more, you can call yourself a Sensitive Striver.

What Makes a Sensitive Striver

Sensitivity is a *personality trait*, not a *disorder*. It's an integral, unchangeable part of who you are, and it comes about through two mechanisms:

1. The first is *nature*, which refers to innate traits like genetics and biology.
2. The second is *nurture*, which refers to upbringing and environment.

NATURE: YOUR GENETIC GIFTS

About 15 to 20 percent of the population has inherited a special set of genes that lead to sensory-processing sensitivity (SPS)—the trait's scientific term—which is another way of saying that you have a highly attuned central nervous system. Studies have shown that sensitive people have more active mental circuitry and neurochemicals in areas related to attention, action-planning, decision-making, and having strong internal experiences. In other words, you have a deep capacity to channel your focus with precision, make thoughtful choices, and spark rich insights to bring great ideas to the table.

Researchers believe that SPS exists and has persisted because it provides an evolutionary advantage. Psychologist Dr. Elaine Aron, who first discovered the trait, has suggested that SPS is an "innate survival strategy," which helped sensitive people cope with the unpredictability of prehistoric times. Pausing and observing—a hallmark of SPS—was invaluable for avoiding predators and staying free from harm. Picking up on environmental cues and recognizing things that less-sensitive people didn't helped those with SPS make wiser decisions and come out ahead in dangerous situations.

While we may no longer need to avoid dangers in the wild, SPS is still an invaluable trait: Managers consistently rate people with higher sensitivity as their top contributors. They are innovative, deeply committed to fairness, and have a knack for leading teams of people in a way others simply can't. At the same time, hyper-attunement to every minor inter-action and inner experience can be frustrating. Situations that might be moderately stressful to the average person can cause a sensitive person to shut down, especially when factors feel out of control. Even the inten-sity of happiness and joy can drain the sensitive mind. That's because when genetically predetermined sensitivity and mental acuity combine, it can lead to being more reactive to the needs of those around you. In fact, a 2015 study published in the *Australian Journal of Psychology* found that high sensitivity is linked to greater feelings of distress because of the way sensitive people internally process emotions. Sensitive people's stress hormones tend to spike when things don't go well, and they have a harder time communicating the impact stress has on them. Worst of all, they tend to default to avoidance or withdrawal to cope, which definitely isn't the healthiest way to resolve conflicts. The researchers also found that sensitive people who didn't deal with their feelings felt more upset and powerless.

NURTURE: THE STIGMA OF SENSITIVITY

Even though genetics is an important piece of the puzzle, your upbring-ing also contributes to how you respond to situations within and around you. From childhood, you may have been told by parents, teachers, and friends to *quit stressing and don't make a fuss* or to *get over yourself* because you're *too high-maintenance*. Now bosses and colleagues tell you that you need to *grow a thicker skin*. Maybe you wonder why others can react calmly and confidently to challenges, when minor situations leave you reeling for days.

Even though your feelings are perfectly normal, you've probably taken these messages to mean that you're not okay as you are, and that you must change in order to be liked and accepted. As a Sensitive Striver, my life was similarly peppered with insecurity and criticism from others and from myself. I grew up feeling like an oddball and came to believe that I was defective. By the time I finished college and graduate school, I had trained myself to hide my real needs and feelings and to only let people see what I thought they wanted to see. Like many Sensitive Strivers, I frequently pushed myself to the brink of burnout trying to live up to the expectations other people had of me and the impossibly high expectations I had of myself. If left unchecked, this tendency can lead you to look outside of yourself to gain approval, rather than sourcing it from within. What's worse is that instead of embracing your sensitivity for the strength and even superpower that it can be, like me, you've probably tried to stifle it as a survival mechanism to fit in. But if you've ever tried this, then you know firsthand that it usually doesn't work. When you reject your true nature, you create a war within yourself.

That's particularly true for women. While current research suggests there are no gender differences in sensitivity between women and men, there are historical and sociological realities that are hard to ignore. For instance, growing up, girls are taught to be accommodating and obedient. By their teens, nearly 45 percent of girls say they are *not allowed* to fail. They react to stress with excessive worrying and by personalizing negative situations—a response that is only exaggerated by the deep thinking and feeling of a Sensitive Striver's brain. Stereotypical beliefs that women should be polite, soft-spoken, and likable can hold them back from asserting themselves and advancing in the workplace at the same pace as their male counterparts. Toxic masculinity, on the other hand, has discouraged men from embracing their innate sensitivity because the trait is often equated with being *soft*. Even though studies show that at infancy, newborn boys are more emotionally reactive than girls, young boys tend to grow up believing manliness is measured by dominance and aggression. As a result, many men spend decades denying their gifts and living lives that don't suit them.

Strategy: Know Yourself

Sensitive striving has many variations, but it shows up most often as one of six core qualities that form the acronym STRIVE. You may easily recognize yourself in some of these descriptions while some of the others might not feel as familiar or relevant. That's okay. The STRIVE qualities exist on a spectrum like any other trait.

Sensitivity. Processing complex information comes naturally to you because you're perceptive and have a heightened response to what's happening within and around you. You thrive best with structure and routine. Without it, you get easily overstimulated, especially if you're under pressure (both real and imagined).

Thoughtfulness. You're highly self-aware, reflective, and intuitive. Your ability to see nuance and to synthesize information makes you especially original and creative. On the flip side, your brain is often racing. It's not uncommon for you to overanalyze day-to-day experiences, and your above-average self-awareness can veer into self-consciousness and self-criticism.

Responsibility. You're dependable and people trust you and look to you for support. Hardworking (perhaps to a fault), you can't bear to let people down, even if it entails sacrifice. A never-ending desire to be liked and to please others is exhausting, contributing to burnout.

Inner Drive. Sensitive Strivers live to exceed expectations, not only on performance reviews, but in every aspect of life. You devote substantial energy to your career and care deeply about making an impact. Nothing makes you more excited than hitting goals or knocking items off your (very long) to-do list, but you often set an unrealistically high bar for success.

Vigilance. You are keenly attuned to changes and tend to be aware of subtleties in your environment, from your boss's body language to the general mood of a meeting. You listen well and try to be responsive to people's needs. Being on high alert can be draining, however, and you may sometimes perceive danger or a threat where there is none.

Emotionality. Sincere and empathetic, you feel things in a big way and have complex emotional responses. You're able to experience the richness of positive emotions like inspiration and gratitude, but can also get stuck in unpleasant feelings like annoyance and disappointment.

STRIVE QUALITY

SENSITIVITY

NOT BALANCED AT ALL	COMPLETELY BALANCED
Anxious and amped up most of the time	Calm and composed demeanor even under pressure
Slow to relax	Get enough time for proper rest and downtime
Body in state of tension and fear	Able to use intuition as a tool for better decision-making

THOUGHTFULNESS

NOT BALANCED AT ALL	COMPLETELY BALANCED
Can't make simple decisions	Reflective and able to think deeply and act purposefully
Plagued by worry and imposter syndrome	Practice constructive self-talk and has solid self-confidence
Get bogged down in unnecessary details	Offer creative, innovative, and nuanced ideas that others miss

RESPONSIBILITY

NOT BALANCED AT ALL	COMPLETELY BALANCED
Swoop in to fix situations and keep people happy	Dedicated, but with strong boundaries
Feel bad or guilty for not doing enough or helping enough	Delegate effectively and empower others to solve problems
Struggle to say no or ask for help	Maintain personal standards for excellence without caving to pressure, comparison, or people-pleasing

STRIVE QUALITY	
INNER DRIVE	
NOT BALANCED AT ALL	COMPLETELY BALANCED
Overwork to the point of exhaustion and burnout	Place a focus on continually learning, growing, and advancing
Take on too many goals and obligations	Create goals that are realistic, attainable, and personally meaningful
High attachment to outcomes and external rewards	Make consistent progress while managing energy effectively
VIGILANCE	
NOT BALANCED AT ALL	COMPLETELY BALANCED
Highly responsive and deferential to the needs of other people	Attunement and empathy with others that create strong relationships
Read into situations, even when there's nothing to worry about	Able to assess risks and make good judgment calls
Passive in interactions	Channel attention inward and pursue what's right for you
EMOTIONALITY	
NOT BALANCED AT ALL	COMPLETELY BALANCED
Derailed by intense, unpleasant feelings for hours or days	Take in positive feelings like joy, pride, and satisfaction without guilt
Pretend everything is okay while silently brooding	Effectively process and work through emotions to take constructive action
At the whim of an ever-changing stream of feelings	Respond to emotions with acceptance and flexibility

While it may seem counterintuitive, these qualities, when taken to an extreme, can actually become a liability. For example, it's great to be detail-oriented, but if you need to read every email ten times before hitting send, your productivity may unwittingly grind to a halt. If you're loyal and caring to an extreme, then personality differences that naturally arise on teams can derail you or prevent you from having boundaries that protect your well-being. That's why it's so important to know yourself, to see how the STRIVE qualities impact your life, and to begin to rebalance any qualities you may be overusing.

Take some time to think about your last month and the reasons you picked up this book. Now look at the scale below and choose a number between one and ten to describe how much you agree or disagree with each statement. Don't overthink it! Just rate yourself honestly (even if you can't give yourself gold stars across the board). This assessment is the first step in figuring out how balanced each of these qualities is in your own life. You'll use these numbers later in the chapter to map out where you are now and to determine where you want to be in the weeks, months, and years to come. After all, knowing yourself isn't about changing who you are or becoming less sensitive and ambitious. Rather, it's actually about channeling your core qualities effectively so you can become who you are meant to be.

STRIVE QUALITIES SCALE

SENSITIVITY

I'm able to stay calm and composed, even under pressure.

COMPLETELY AGREE 10 9 8 7 6 5 4 3 2 1 SOMEWHAT AGREE

I get enough downtime and rest.

COMPLETELY AGREE 10 9 8 7 6 5 4 3 2 1 SOMEWHAT AGREE

I'm satisfied with the habits and routines I use to manage my energy.

COMPLETELY AGREE 10 9 8 7 6 5 4 3 2 1 SOMEWHAT AGREE

THOUGHTFULNESS

I make decisions without getting bogged down in unnecessary details.

COMPLETELY AGREE 10 9 8 7 6 5 4 3 2 1 SOMEWHAT AGREE

I don't let insecurities and doubts distract me from the task at hand.

COMPLETELY AGREE 10 9 8 7 6 5 4 3 2 1 SOMEWHAT AGREE

I'm able to tune out other thoughts so I can concentrate, focus, and get into a deep flow when I work.

COMPLETELY AGREE 10 9 8 7 6 5 4 3 2 1 SOMEWHAT AGREE

STRIVE QUALITIES SCALE

RESPONSIBILITY

I delegate tasks effectively and ask for help when I need it.

COMPLETELY AGREE 10 9 8 7 6 5 4 3 2 1 SOMEWHAT AGREE

When I make a promise to myself, I generally keep it and follow through.

COMPLETELY AGREE 10 9 8 7 6 5 4 3 2 1 SOMEWHAT AGREE

I'm able to diplomatically say no to projects, people, and situations without worrying that I'm being rude or mean.

COMPLETELY AGREE 10 9 8 7 6 5 4 3 2 1 SOMEWHAT AGREE

INNER DRIVE

I spend most of my time on high-value work.

COMPLETELY AGREE 10 9 8 7 6 5 4 3 2 1 SOMEWHAT AGREE

I create goals based on what sounds fun, exciting, or inspiring to me.

COMPLETELY AGREE 10 9 8 7 6 5 4 3 2 1 SOMEWHAT AGREE

My goals are realistic and attainable given my other obligations.

COMPLETELY AGREE 10 9 8 7 6 5 4 3 2 1 SOMEWHAT AGREE

VIGILANCE

I balance my own needs with those of the people around me.

COMPLETELY AGREE 10 9 8 7 6 5 4 3 2 1 SOMEWHAT AGREE

I take calculated-but-smart risks in my career that help me advance.

COMPLETELY AGREE 10 9 8 7 6 5 4 3 2 1 SOMEWHAT AGREE

I'm mindful and selective about my work environment so that I create conditions that work best for me.

COMPLETELY AGREE 10 9 8 7 6 5 4 3 2 1 SOMEWHAT AGREE

EMOTIONALITY

I don't take feedback or criticism personally.

COMPLETELY AGREE 10 9 8 7 6 5 4 3 2 1 SOMEWHAT AGREE

I'm able to gain distance and perspective from my emotional reactions.

COMPLETELY AGREE 10 9 8 7 6 5 4 3 2 1 SOMEWHAT AGREE

Bad moods generally don't phase me for too long.

COMPLETELY AGREE 10 9 8 7 6 5 4 3 2 1 SOMEWHAT AGREE

Get Unstuck

1. PRACTICE SEEING YOUR ACTIONS THROUGH THE STRIVE LENS. If you have trouble rating yourself at first, don't worry. As you go about your business over the next few days, notice tasks and situations you approach with confidence versus those you struggle with. Then ask yourself what STRIVE qualities are at play in either scenario.

2. BUILD A SUPPORTIVE COMMUNITY. What was once an invisible trait can now be a helpful framework for others to understand you better. Tell your family, close friends, and trusted coworkers that you're a Sensitive Striver and introduce them to the STRIVE qualities. Support is crucial, and these conversations can provide valuable insight about how your STRIVE qualities are balanced or unbalanced. You may also discover that others are Sensitive Strivers, too.

3. FOCUS ON WHAT'S WORKING. The traditional approach to problem-solving is to focus on the negative and to try and fix what's wrong. Instead, tune into when you are your best possible self and remind yourself how and why your STRIVE qualities are an asset.

Strategy in Action: Kelly

During our first conversation, Kelly told me about the past year and what had led her to call me. Taking a medical leave was something she had never imagined doing, and she felt surprised and dismayed that the time she spent away from work hadn't been enough to resolve her challenges. She was worried that if something didn't change, she might have to leave a field that she loved or to further sacrifice her health, but she didn't know where to start and was unsure of how to describe exactly what was wrong. I assured Kelly that there was nothing to *fix* and introduced her to the STRIVE qualities. Before our second conversation, I asked Kelly to complete the STRIVE Qualities Scale that you saw earlier in this chapter.

In our next meeting, Kelly said she was able to put words to her feelings and struggles for the first time; the STRIVE framework was the information she needed to begin to think about a change. It was a breakthrough for Kelly to comprehend that she wasn't broken—she simply needed to manage herself differently. Realizing she couldn't hold herself to the same expectations as others allowed her to step back and to see the bigger picture so she could assess and prioritize where she wanted to make changes for the better.

When Kelly examined her STRIVE qualities, she noticed a few areas in which she rated herself low, but she was particularly concerned by how her unbalanced Thoughtfulness contributed to negative self-talk, like blaming herself for not keeping up with the workload and telling herself to work harder. As we discussed her Thoughtfulness further, she was able to view it as an asset, especially when the agency needed innovative ways to reach its target communities. Her bigger realization, however, was that her STRIVE qualities were exactly what made her a stellar performer and collaborator in an organization that desperately needed a dedicated leader. Her difficulties weren't arising because she was incapable, but rather because she was applying her STRIVE qualities in ways that weren't serving her.

Kelly committed to seeing herself in a new light, and even though the result of the actions she hoped to make wouldn't be instantaneous, she realized she had the ability to tip the scales and to reapply her STRIVE qualities in ways that leveraged the upsides and mitigated the downsides. As one of her initial steps, she sat down with a trusted colleague and explained that she was feeling overwhelmed again. He was surprised to hear this since Kelly was always the first to step up when it came time to take on extra responsibilities. Together, the two decided that during the next six months they would bring discipline to the agency's overflowing workload, putting together new project plans that included a compelling case for hiring more staff. Even though Kelly was nervous about asking for help, she knew that if she was truly going to be able to use her STRIVE qualities in new ways, she would have to be open to doing things differently and to get comfortable with not knowing exactly how it would work out.

Most importantly, she began to put into practice the same techniques you will discover throughout the rest of this book, including quieting her inner critic, accepting her emotions, and learning how to advocate for herself. While the path wasn't perfectly linear, as you'll see in Chapter Nine, within a few months of returning to work, Kelly was able to think about her career more objectively with an eye to understanding (and protecting) her sensitivity, using it to her advantage, and channeling her drive in healthier, more sustainable ways.

THE WHEEL OF BALANCE

The Wheel of Balance is a visual way to determine how balanced or unbalanced your STRIVE qualities are and where to focus first. I've included Kelly's Wheel of Balance for you as an example. Keep yours in a safe place because we will come back to it in subsequent chapters.

INSTRUCTIONS

1. *Give yourself a score.* Remember the STRIVE Qualities Scale you completed earlier? Take the average of your answers to get a number for each of the qualities. Each slice on your Wheel of Balance represents how balanced you are in that particular STRIVE quality right now.

2. *Pinpoint your current reality.* Draw a line across the slice and shade it in (see the following image for an example).

3. *Identify your desired reality.* Rate each area on your wheel based on how balanced you want to be six months in the future. Draw a dashed line across the slices.

4. *Give the overall picture a gut check.* Adjust scores if they don't feel right, but don't increase your score because you think it should be higher.

5. *Gauge your growth gap.* The difference between your shaded section and the dashed line is your growth gap. Write the difference between the two numbers outside each slice. Some areas will have larger growth gaps than others. What aspects are you motivated to work on first as you read the rest of this book? The goal isn't to achieve perfect balance, but rather to assess whether you are moving *toward* or *away* from balance.

THE WHEEL OF BALANCE

Kelly

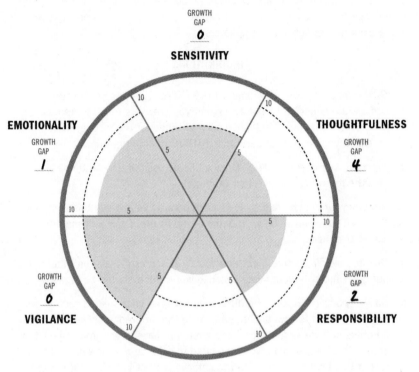

	GROWTH GAP
Sensitivity	0
Thoughtfulness	4
Responsibility	2
Inner Drive	2
Vigilance	0
Emotionality	1

THE WHEEL OF BALANCE

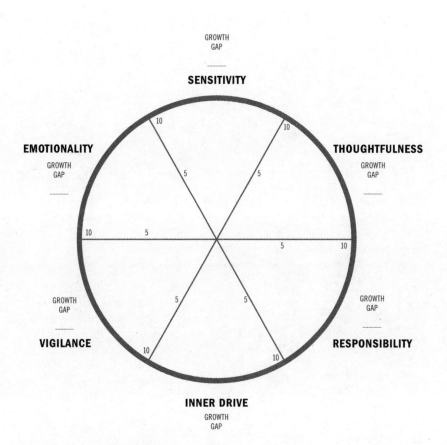

	GROWTH GAP
Sensitivity	
Thoughtfulness	
Responsibility	
Inner Drive	
Vigilance	
Emotionality	

OVERCOME THE HONOR ROLL HANGOVER

2

"When we grow and shift and transform, we are
not becoming better . . . we are simply returning
to what we have always been."

—LISA OLIVERA

IT WAS 1 P.M. ON FRIDAY, AND ALICIA sat at the kitchen counter, distractedly clicking between thirteen different job posting tabs in her web browser. *If I make a change now, I'll have to start all over*, she thought to herself. *But if I don't take the leap soon, I'll probably be stuck doing this forever.* As senior sales representative at a major magazine, Alicia knew she had the kind of job other people envied. She earned a six-figure income and had great perks like work-from-home Fridays and an extended maternity leave, benefits she needed now more than ever as she planned to have a child on her own. Just then, her sister entered the kitchen to make a cup of tea. "Are you hungover?" she asked. Alicia shook her head. She hadn't been out drinking the night before. This was an Honor Roll Hangover.

Seventeen years before, Alicia had enthusiastically embarked on a career in advertising. Hardworking and sensitive, she had been steadily promoted, and her salary had gone up and up even as her excitement about selling dwindled. From the outside, it looked like Alicia had *made it*, but over the years, she came to regret her decision (and beat herself up about it all the time). She frequently wondered if she was wasting the most important years of her career on work she no longer found interesting or meaningful. Alicia had always been good at creating and maintaining relationships, but on a personal level, she found herself lonely at the office because her cliquey coworkers left her out of team lunches and after-work happy hours. She was still proud of her rise from intern to senior sales rep, but Alicia had come to despise the fact that she was only as valuable to the company as the new business she brought in. "The constant pressure to land big deals is exhausting, not exhilarating," she told me when we first met, and that pressure was increasing by the day as a recession set in and her company considered layoffs.

It was obvious Alicia needed a change, but all she could think about was how her confusion and hopelessness were a far cry from the energy and determination she used to feel when she approached a challenge. The Inner Drive that had once served her so well now kept her pushing toward goals that she no longer cared about, and yet her amped-up Vigilance prevented her from making a change because she was so worried about what others might think or whether she would be able to make a move given the state of the economy. She knew she had so much potential, yet felt like she was letting herself down.

After years of succeeding following paths laid out for her, Alicia, like many Sensitive Strivers, was a master at doing what she *should* do. Many Sensitive Strivers spend their entire adult lives in a sort of performance, showing up as the people they *think* they need to be in order to be successful. I see it all the time with my clients: Whether they're burning out trying to get a first promotion or leading large teams across the globe, they, like Alicia, struggle with indecision and a lack of self-trust despite their accomplishments.

To feel worthy, Sensitive Strivers try to capture self-esteem by chasing external validation, promotions, accolades, and approval. They believe (unconsciously) that if they could just put in more effort they'd feel *good enough*, so they work harder and longer in order to compensate for their perceived failings. Without inner stability, they're forced to gain confidence from sources outside themselves. The thrill of achievement may be temporarily satisfying, but when the high inevitably wears off, these Sensitive Strivers are left with a sinking sense of dissatisfaction and exhaustion. This cycle is emblematic of something I call the Honor Roll Hangover, a messy mix of perfectionism, people-pleasing, and overfunctioning that leads Sensitive Strivers to become addicted to achievement.

The Worst Hangover of Your Life

The Honor Roll Hangover isn't the kind of hangover that you fix with a bacon, egg, and cheese sandwich. It's a form of achievement addiction that follows Sensitive Strivers from childhood into the workplace. This kind of *hangover* results in the same anxiety, fatigue, and emptiness you might feel after a night of drinking too much, but it comes about when the beliefs and actions that once helped you excel in the classroom start to hold you back and cost you your inner peace.

Without a doubt, the Honor Roll Hangover is the biggest obstacle my clients face when they're learning to trust themselves. But once they do unhinge their self-worth from their achievements, they realize they can seek meaning from being productive and invested in their work without being controlled by it.

The Honor Roll Hangover tends to show up in the following ways:

- **You're fixated on goal-setting.** You enjoy setting goals, and you set lots of them, often to the point where you feel lost without targets to hit. If you hit your goal, you're worthy. If you don't, you're worthless.

- **If you're not the best, you're not good enough.** All your life, you've strived to be perfect—at school, in extracurriculars, and now at work. To you, anything less than an A-plus feels like failure. Just meeting expectations on your performance review feels like getting an F on a test and makes you want to crawl into bed for days.

- **You feel like an imposter.** Despite your education, training, and experience, you feel like you don't know as much as your colleagues or peers—this is called imposter syndrome. You worry you'll speak in an uninformed way or raise your hand to offer a foolish idea that will expose you as the fraud you believe you are.

- **You focus on doing things *the right way*.** You insist on dotting i's and crossing t's on every single task or else it doesn't sit right with you. Attention to detail is important to you (even if you're not being graded on it anymore).

- **You push yourself to work harder—not necessarily smarter.** You're never satisfied with yourself, most notably when you're treating yourself to downtime, which you probably view as wasteful or undeserved. You feel like you're *not doing enough* unless your schedule is packed with obligations.

- **You crave gold stars.** You expect—and are disappointed by not getting—a pat on the back for your efforts from your boss, colleagues, or other important people in your life.

- **You beat yourself up when you make a mistake.** You have a hard time bouncing back after slipping up even if it doesn't have a larger effect on your career. And you tend to feel shame, as opposed to guilt, when you make an error. Shame says, *I am bad* (which suggests a character flaw) whereas guilt says, *I did something wrong* (which suggests it's within your control to fix or improve).

- **Your emotions feel like a runaway train.** Emotionality is a fact of life for Sensitive Strivers, but the Honor Roll Hangover can lead you to feel *hypersensitive*—making you self-critical and reactive to daily stressors, inconveniences, or feedback. You may often feel moody for no apparent reason.

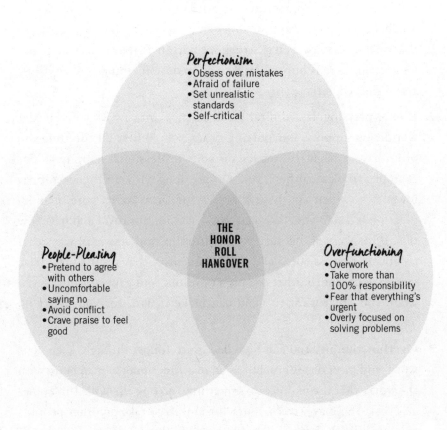

THREE ELEMENTS THAT DRIVE THE HONOR ROLL HANGOVER

The Honor Roll Hangover comes down to three key behaviors:

1. **Perfectionism.** Perfectionism leads you to overemphasize your weaknesses and underestimate your strengths. This can look like obsessing over mistakes and always feeling like you have to *prove* yourself. But here's the thing: Perfectionism isn't really about being flawless (you

probably realize that's not possible, anyway). Beneath the surface, it's actually a coping mechanism to control or distract yourself from fear. You believe you must appear shiny and impeccable on the outside, so that no one sees how you're struggling within. Perfectionism also convinces you there is only one *right* way to do something, and anything else is unacceptable.

2. **People-pleasing.** It's admirable to be a pleasant coworker or a leader who lends support, but putting other people first all the time can often have a negative impact on your professional happiness. For example, to please others, you may go along with colleagues' subpar ideas, even when you have a better solution. At its core, people-pleasing is a sign you have a strong desire for approval and have low regard for *yourself*, because you're thinking and acting in ways that compromise your core values. The insecurity that results may drive you to conform to other people's opinions and expectations—even when you don't want to—and can make it hard for you to say no when you should.

3. **Overfunctioning.** You can be relied on to follow through, keep your word, and meet deadlines. But as an overfunctioner, you operate with the worry that if you don't do something, no one else will. This comes at a cost. You may stretch yourself too thin or take on other people's responsibilities as your own, like working late nights and weekends to cover for your team. You may even try to assume responsibility for other people's reactions (which, spoiler alert, is impossible). The psychological load can be unbearably draining. Beyond exhaustion, one of the biggest problems with overfunctioning is that it creates an unhealthy dynamic that allows other people to *underfunction*. When you assume responsibility for *fixing* situations and rescuing other people, they don't have to do their part, which can be frustrating at best and damaging at worst.

Why *Fake It Till You Make It* Doesn't Work

Without the tools to deal with the Honor Roll Hangover, many Sensitive Strivers have to work hard to hide their feelings of inadequacy. And when that doesn't work, they try to *fake it till they make it* and push feelings of self-doubt away in hopes that they'll reach a point where they finally feel good enough. The Honor Roll Hangover tricks us into thinking we can earn approval and worthiness if only we check enough boxes or meet minimum requirements and prerequisites, which isn't reasonable or possible. It's not how the working world, well, *works*. Operating in your career constantly striving for A-pluses is not only futile, it's also harmful. It can drive you to burn out, and more importantly, it drives you further away from what's important and best for you.

Anne Helen Petersen is one woman whose desire to *win* at her career and adulthood drove her straight to burnout. As she wrote for *BuzzFeed*, ". . . I've internalized the idea that I should be working all the time. . . . Because everything and everyone in my life has reinforced it—explicitly and implicitly—since I was young." Anne's Honor Roll Hangover showed itself as weariness and an inability to dial down the compulsion to do and achieve, regardless of the consequences. She began to notice that while she could skillfully balance multiple work assignments, her finances, health, and a cross-country move, for weeks she would neglect other basic tasks that would have made her life outside of work easier or better, like making doctor's appointments or emailing friends. Anne felt a sense of shame and simply couldn't brush off her procrastination like other people could. As she dug deeper into the imbalance between her professional and personal lives, Anne realized it wasn't lack of desire or time; it was the result of decades of trying to "achieve the end goal of 1) a *good* job that would 2) be or sound cool and 3) allow [her] to follow [her] *passion*." She'd been raised to approach life and her career as a series of competitions as opposed to a state of being, learning, and evolving.

Anne and the experiences of countless Sensitive Strivers support research that shows that it's possible to develop an unhealthy dependence on achievement. Your brain quite literally becomes addicted to the rush of *feel-good* chemicals you get from external validation, pursuing new heights, and making other people happy. Like a drug, you need to keep performing in order to get your fix, but even though our culture glorifies workaholism, it isn't good for us. Social media keeps us connected and comparing ourselves to our friends' highlight reels. The pressure to keep up and avoid falling behind can lead to anxiety and depression, low self-esteem, and worse work performance. And the higher you climb, the further you fall: Studies show that higher-income workers experience more stress and neglect downtime—which isn't good news for their well-being.

Many Sensitive Strivers try to resolve their Honor Roll Hangover with so-called self-care and life hacks, which only provide temporary relief (and may actually contribute to the problem). To tackle the root cause, you need to recognize when your desire to achieve is no longer serving you.

Strategy: Give Up Goals

Having grand ambitions and goals *aren't* the problem. What's unhealthy is how the Honor Roll Hangover triggers you to *relate* to them and your *motivation* for pursuing them, all of which ultimately drives an imbalance in your STRIVE qualities. Moving from the Honor Roll Hangover to trusting yourself, then, requires evaluating when and why your ambitions no longer serve you, so you can release what's not working and create more room for what will. Here's how to discern when you may need to rethink a goal or priority—or let it go altogether.

- **When the goal wasn't yours in the first place.** If you want a promotion because you're excited to grow, great. But if you're working your way up the ladder just because you're driven by a sense of competition or obligation, check yourself. Telltale signs your Responsibility and Vigilance are off balance include saying to yourself you *should, have to, or need to* pursue something versus *wanting to*. Signing up for a half-marathon because everyone at the office is doing it is very different than registering because you crave the physical challenge. The former is influenced by fear of missing out, while the latter is an inner longing.

- **When the goal brings you more distress than benefit.** Nothing is fun all the time, no matter how much you love it. It's also normal for your goals to feel a little bit scary and for you to be nervous about whether you can accomplish them or not. But some negative feelings go beyond a healthy sense of trepidation and bring profound dread, sleepless nights, or other health consequences. These are little (or big) nudges from your Emotionality and Sensitivity that the Honor Roll Hangover is at play. For example, your stomach may lurch at the thought of spending your entire workday on client services, even though it sounds cool to someone else.

- **When you're more fixated on the results than the process.** Your Thoughtfulness can turn into rigidity, and when this happens you may get so caught up in achieving and pleasing that you fail to consider whether or not you actually *want* to acquire the skills you need to reach a goal in the first place. For example, you may set your sights on growing your business to one million dollars a year, but secretly, you don't really want what comes with a company that size (like building a team, managing budgets, etc.).

- **When you're abandoning yourself.** You're likely to outgrow certain dreams, but an unchecked commitment to follow through at all costs can keep you stuck to outdated priorities despite the fact that your enthusiasm has disappeared. When your STRIVE quality of Inner Drive is unbalanced, goals can become all-consuming, and soon you can find yourself neglecting your well-being in the name of getting things done.

Get Unstuck

1. FOCUS ON WHAT YOU STAND TO GAIN. It takes courage to let go of what's not working. Rather than focusing on what you're losing, hone in on what giving up goals affords you, like more time and energy. Remember no decision is permanent. You can continue to make adjustments until you find the balance of goals that works for you.

2. PRIORITIZE RUTHLESSLY. In one of my coaching programs, clients experimented with cutting their to-do lists by 70 percent, and the results were remarkable. One member launched a new business revenue stream. Another started working on a book he had been promising himself he would write for years. Shrinking their lists forced them to trim the fat and get rid of any tasks that weren't essential.

3. CURE YOUR COMPARISON. In the throes of the Honor Roll Hangover, you may find yourself constantly comparing yourself to others. Jealousy can be useful and guide you to an under-recognized desire to possess or experience something that you don't currently. What secret wish or desire do you want to give voice to?

4. LET GO OF OPPORTUNITY FOMO. A fear of missing out when it comes to professional and career development can drive you to say yes to every future meeting, conference, or assignment, justifying it by saying this may be a potential *big break* or valuable way to make connections. I find that asking myself, *If this event or commitment were tomorrow, would I be excited about it?* helps me stay true to my own needs and desires in the moment.

Strategy in Action: Alicia

When Alicia stepped back and thought about her professional life and the objectives that had guided her, she realized that climbing the ladder was making her miserable. Not only was her energy for work at an all-time low, but her Vigilance was on overdrive, and she was consumed by what people, especially her coworkers, would think if she quit her job and then had a baby on her own. Her anxiety was so draining that she had also stopped going to the gym and had quit doing pottery—two hobbies that used to bring her joy.

Although it felt unnatural at first, Alicia decided to rebalance her Inner Drive by taking a hiatus from job searching *and* by slowing down the frenetic pace she usually kept as she bounced between new business and client service. She talked to her boss about scaling back her monthly quota so that she could focus on client maintenance, something that was important as her big accounts considered decreasing their advertising budgets. With the time she recaptured, she rebuilt lost habits that made her feel good about herself, starting with reregistering for her ceramics class. She also made a point to schedule a weekly lunch or dinner with her sister or a friend so she would have something social to look forward to.

Over the course of eight weeks, these small changes helped Alicia detox from her Honor Roll Hangover, and she felt more optimistic about her future and more like herself again. Best of all, with renewed mental and emotional clarity, she was able to reclaim enough breathing room to reconsider how her professional goals might dovetail with her personal goals and strengths. In Chapter Ten, we'll return to Alicia and how she redefined what was important to her and moved ahead.

Like Alicia, recognizing your Honor Roll Hangover can be a new beginning, if you let it be, because it gives you the nudge you need to be truer to yourself. Giving up goals can be a call to arms to stop living life on autopilot. So on days where you feel depleted, unmotivated, or unmoored, return to yourself. Treat those feelings with curiosity, explore where the Honor Roll Hangover may be coming into play, and respond from a place of self-compassion so that everything can shift for the better.

FIVE-DAY
HONOR ROLL HANGOVER
DETOX

Taking inventory of how you spend your time is a straightforward way to understand how you're letting perfectionism, people-pleasing, and overfunctioning control your life. The data will reveal where you need to let go of certain expectations and obligations so you can free up energy to reinvest in yourself and reclaim a sense of agency.

INSTRUCTIONS

1. *Track your time.* For the next five days, document how you spend your time using the tracker provided. Be specific—an eight-hour block labeled *work* is too broad. Instead, note particular projects or meetings. Aim to track in one-hour increments. You'll have to be more granular if you find yourself hopping between tasks. It may be a pain, but your well-being is worth it.

2. *Reflect on instances of the Honor Roll Hangover.* Signs to look for are that the task . . .

   • Caused you to feel distressed or self-conscious
   • Brought up a sense of obligation, pressure, or urgency
   • Is something you didn't feel right about doing, but you did anyway
   • Feels like something you *have to* or *should do*

   Worried that all of your entries meet these criteria? The tools in this book will help you make major changes.

3. *Make a change.* Pick one low-risk task or commitment to delete from your to-do list, approach differently, delegate, or scale back effort on. Try the one that feels like the easiest, or that you have the most influence over. For example, instead of forcing yourself to *be productive* and respond to emails when you wake up, listen to an audiobook. Move on to giving up more tiny tasks over the next thirty days. What may seem like micro-steps will add up to big results.

FIVE-DAY
HONOR ROLL HANGOVER
DETOX
Alicia

HONOR ROLL HANGOVER DETOX

DATE: February 4 — IF THE HONOR ROLL HANGOVER IS AT PLAY, COMPLETE THE FOLLOWING

TIME	ACTIVITY	HOW DID IT MANIFEST?	WHAT CHANGE WILL I MAKE?	WHAT DOES THIS PROVIDE OR ALLOW ME TO DO?
6–7:45	Morning routine	Felt bad about myself as I looked at social media while eating breakfast.	Watch an inspirational video instead of scrolling my feeds.	Nourish my mind and do something for myself before the workday starts.
8–9	Daily team meeting	I caved and committed to a bigger quota than I felt comfortable with because my boss suggested it.	Talk to my boss next week about scaling it back to something more reasonable.	I'm relieved that it means I won't have to travel as much.
9–11:30	Client Appt			
12–1:15	Lunch break	Worked through lunch because I wanted to keep the client happy and turn around a proposal quickly.	Make plans to have lunch with my sister or take time to sketch what I plan to make at ceramics this week.	I can decompress and enjoy my lunch!
1:30–2:30	Deck for maintaining client revenue			
3–4:30	Lead generation	Set up a half dozen meetings for coming weeks because I felt pressure to keep up, and immediately dreaded them.	Limit the time I spend on lead generation to half an hour per day.	I can redirect my time and energy to working with the creative teams, which I find fun and enjoyable.
5–5:45	Evening walk	I agonized over an email to a client trying to find the right words to say. Why was I even writing an email anyway! This is supposed to be "me time."	Delete my work email from my phone before I leave the house so I'm not tempted to check it.	I can listen to my favorite podcast or to a meditation.
6–7	Ceramics class			
7:30–8:30	Dinner			
9–10:30	Job searching	Tried to make progress on my resume but felt like I have no accomplishments. Went down a rabbit hole looking at job boards.	STOP! I promised to take a hiatus.	It frees up lots of time for me to do more art.
11–11:30	Nighttime routine			

FIVE-DAY
HONOR ROLL HANGOVER
DETOX

HONOR ROLL HANGOVER DETOX				
DATE:		IF THE HONOR ROLL HANGOVER IS AT PLAY, COMPLETE THE FOLLOWING		
TIME	ACTIVITY	HOW DID IT MANIFEST?	WHAT CHANGE WILL I MAKE?	WHAT DOES THIS PROVIDE OR ALLOW ME TO DO?

GIVE YOURSELF PERMISSION

3

"Don't wait to be praised, anointed, or validated. Don't wait for someone to give you permission to lead."

—TARA MOHR

IF YOU'VE DONE THE EXERCISE IN CHAPTER TWO, you know that giving up goals that don't serve you anymore can free up time and mental space. But that's only the first step toward creating a more intentional life focused on achievement that's meaningful to you and that leverages your STRIVE qualities. The next step is to give yourself permission to explore and to act in ways you want to instead of sourcing approval from outside of yourself.

Permission-seeking is instinctive. Everyone has an innate desire to be liked and to belong. It's normal to want to avoid the pain of rejection, judgment, or failure. Besides, external validation isn't *all* bad. It can be fulfilling to know your contribution is critical to a project's success or to relish getting rewarded for being awesome at your job. But for Sensitive Strivers, seeking approval can escalate from a *desire* to a *dependency*. Many of my clients struggle with this distinction early on, and Travis was no different.

Before he even sat down, Travis handed me a sheet of paper with "Business Pricing Matrix" scribbled at the top. "This is the year I earn my first hundred dollars in my own business," he said. "Here, check this out."

My eyes glazed over as I took in the complex spreadsheet. Travis spent his days as a computer programmer at a hospital, and for the last eighteen months, he had wanted to start a side gig. In his spare time, Travis was a distance runner and had been blogging about running since college. He had toyed with the idea of becoming a running coach or helping a friend with the tech side of a new running shoe company, but after working through the process of giving up goals, he had decided to table the other ideas and to focus on starting a technology consulting business instead.

In classic Sensitive Striver fashion, Travis had approached his entrepreneurial venture with diligence. He specialized in a coding language that was in high demand. He spent hours researching the steps involved in starting a business, analyzed the market, and joined online communities for side hustlers in hopes of seeking more information and inspiration. He even talked things over with his partner, who was supportive. But after almost a year of *preparing*, Travis was still stuck, which is when he came to work with me. I slid the matrix across the table back to Travis. "Before we dive into your pricing plan, let me ask you something. You have a pretty strong network, right?"

"Yeah, people seek out my advice all the time," Travis said. "I know I can capitalize on that and generate good side income, but before I reach out to my contacts to ask for business, I need to make sure I have my ducks in a row." He pointed at the matrix.

"Why?" I asked.

"Well, because that's how you're *supposed* to do it."

Right away, it had become clear that Travis's Honor Roll Hangover was running the show, *big time*. Travis explained he had always been encouraged to follow rules and had been praised for meeting parental expectations. He fully realized this made him a pleaser, yet he had never connected the dots to see that the need for approval he'd learned early on also led him to avoid taking leaps in his career unless he was 100 percent sure he'd do it *right*. As an adult, his Responsibility had pretty much been unbalanced since his first day on the job, from minor issues like overpreparing for every meeting to checking and rechecking his code to make sure it was *correct* despite being a recognized industry expert. Now, because of the Honor Roll Hangover, he was determined to follow a formula for starting his business and had dedicated many hours of his valuable time to planning a complicated pricing structure before earning a single dollar from his new venture.

Clients like Travis come to me all the time wanting to grow their businesses, perform better in their jobs, or feel more proud of who they are and the work they do. While the exact nature of their challenges differs, they're all essentially asking the same underlying question: "How do I stop doubting myself?" In other words, they are *seeking permission* to trust themselves and to find new ways to be in the world that aren't wholly governed by external expectations. It may be the first time in a long time (or ever!) that you've allowed yourself that kind of freedom. Embracing it fully starts by examining the sneaky ways you're currently giving your power away, then releasing yourself from the limiting expectations and roadblocks in your way so you can move forward with conviction.

Give Yourself Permission to . . .

Let's establish a working definition of what it means to give yourself permission to guide you for the rest of this book and to help you get out of your own way. Consider how much you need to give yourself permission in the following areas:

Give yourself permission to . . . **succeed.** Out of a desire to be liked, perhaps you've held yourself back from your full potential. You may fear outshining others, showing off, or stepping on people's toes. But playing small doesn't serve anyone, especially yourself. Remember that there's no one *right* way to accomplish something; there's only the way that feels right for you. Take matters into your own hands and allow yourself to think independently. Giving yourself permission to succeed also means starting something new before you feel completely qualified or prepared.

Give yourself permission to . . . **make mistakes.** A mistake is not a failure. To be imperfect is to be human and there's wisdom to be gained when things don't go as planned. Instead of dwelling on what went wrong (easier said than done, I know!), forgive yourself and acknowledge that you did the best you could with the information and resources you had at the time. Embrace an attitude of experimentation where there are no missteps; there is only learning.

Give yourself permission to . . . **be who you are.** Have patience when finding ways to exercise your STRIVE qualities productively. This can mean making Emotionality your competitive advantage, tapping into your intuition, or setting goals differently to honor your Inner Drive. Don't change your convictions because of another person's doubts. Your preferences, choices, and ambitions are worthwhile and important. Accept yourself for where you are right now, instead of berating yourself over where you ought to be.

FROM WHERE DO YOU SEEK PERMISSION?

OUTSIDE YOURSELF	WITHIN YOURSELF
Wait to be asked or wait for opportunities to be presented to you	Create opportunities where you see a chance to contribute
Hold back out of fear of disapproval or imposter syndrome	Voice your ideas even when you don't feel 100 percent qualified
Need to be liked or told you're competent and good	Act from a place of integrity by setting your own standards and goals
Worry about losing recognition (e.g., praise, money, promotion)	Value the gains in character from making mistakes
Belittle or reevaluate your thoughts and emotions based on others' opinions	Respect yourself and feel entitled to experience your thoughts and feelings

SNEAKY WAYS PERMISSION-SEEKING STEALS YOUR POWER

Seeking awards and accolades is an obvious and often unproductive way to try to bolster your sense of self-worth. But permission-seeking can seep into your habits in other sneaky ways.

Overapologizing. Saying sorry when it's not necessary is a subconscious way to get reassurance that you are okay and allowed to exist.

This includes situations like starting an email with, *I'm sorry to bother you, but . . .* or saying, *Sorry! Let me move over* when someone sits next to you on a bus. When you say *I'm sorry*, are you hoping someone will say, *Nothing to apologize for—you're good* or, *Oh no, you did a great job on that presentation?*

Outsourcing decision-making. When you have to make a decision, do you poll other people or stall until you get outside input? By doing so you're abdicating responsibility, teaching yourself that other people's opinions are more important than your own, and essentially saying, *Tell me what you think is best for me.* This suggests you don't think your judgments are valuable, valid, or worthwhile unless other people agree.

Qualifying and questioning your contributions. Prefacing everything you say with, *I'm not sure if this is a good idea, but . . .* or, *I'm not an expert . . .* can point to an underlying belief that you don't feel qualified or good enough. Similarly, letting phrases like, *Am I making sense?* or, *That's okay, right?* leak into your language undermines your impact (more on that in Chapter Twelve). It also signals that you don't have faith in your ideas, which doesn't inspire trust.

These habits may seem minor, but they are representative of ways you seek approval, which takes you further away from trusting yourself.

Don't Wait to Be Called On

Fran Hauser, media executive and author of *The Myth of the Nice Girl: Achieving a Career You Love without Becoming a Person You Hate*, is someone who embodies what it means to be sensitive and successful without depending on external validation. In the late 1990s, while Fran was working at Moviefone, a company that provided an automated service to buy movie tickets, she realized the company was missing out on a big revenue opportunity. They had been so focused on selling advertising to movie theaters that they were leaving money on the table by not selling to other brands. Fran wanted to create a team to focus on this, but she worried that taking initiative would ruffle feathers.

Many Sensitive Strivers have been in Fran's shoes. Perhaps you've come up with an idea in a meeting, only to second-guess whether you'll sound smart or creative enough if you present it. Or maybe you've spent so much time trying to prepare and perfect a strategy that, like Travis, you stalled for weeks or months. In Fran's case, she didn't wait for her boss to assign a team to her; instead she took initiative. Fran assumed Responsibility and exercised Thoughtfulness in a productive way, consulting with her Chief Revenue Officer and the head of research to put together a plan. Her plan was so solid that her boss gave her the go-ahead to create a two-person team that would unlock ad revenue from other brands. Fran eventually helped lead Moviefone to a $400 million sale to AOL and was later promoted to Vice President and General Manager of Moviefone and AOL Movies in 2001. Fran's story shows that, if you really want to make an impact, you can't wait to be called on. You must trust your judgment and create opportunities for yourself.

Strategy: Start Before You're Ready

Waiting until you feel ready may feel like the safe option, but it's actually a losing bet. So how do you stop doubting yourself and give yourself the permission you need to succeed, make mistakes, and be who you are? The secret is to just start, specifically to start *before* you feel ready.

The challenge is to be okay with the concept of taking *imperfect action* and to trust your ability to figure out the details as you go. Instead of waiting to feel ready, we need to reverse the equation: To trust yourself, you must stop overthinking and start doing. Proving to yourself you can persevere is how you build inner strength. So it's essential you start *now* to become the person you admire.

Imperfect action is not only a process you will use for the rest of this book to change the habits and beliefs that have held you back, but it is also a way of life you can use to approach all of your goals and dreams now and for years to come. It's the essential ingredient that will allow you to approach yourself differently without letting excuses or judgment stop you. If you find yourself hesitating or paralyzed by concerns about what's to come, try to:

- **Focus on your *very next best step*.** What one thing could you do today that would take you nearer to your goal? It's much easier to wrap your head around and take action toward a single next step rather than trying to project months or years into the future. It also helps future-proof your life because you're taking action from a place of agility, not rigid perfectionism.

- **Swap procrasti-learning for just-in-time learning.** The tendency to endlessly seek out more information—taking ten online courses, listening to every podcast—can actually be a Sensitive Striver diversion tactic I call procrasti-learning. Knowledge is useless without action, so start embracing just-in-time learning. This means acquiring knowledge when you need it, for example, if your job duties change, rather than hoarding knowledge for (false) comfort.

- **Root into your resilience.** Whenever I have a client struggling to start before they're ready, I ask them to tell me about the three hardest things they've overcome. They don't need to be directly related to the goal or task at hand. Simply reminding yourself that you can rise above challenges gives you confidence to be greater than your fears and apprehensions. You can bring your courage to the forefront by reflecting on questions like:

  - When I've gone through challenging times, what helped me through it?

  - If I were the bravest version of myself today, what would I be doing?

  - If I knew I couldn't fail, what would I do now?

  - What positive aspects of my STRIVE qualities can I leverage to move forward?

Are there risks with starting before you're ready? Yes, and that's the point. Confidence is not a prerequisite for success; it's a byproduct of taking risks and acting imperfectly. That's why starting before you're ready means putting one foot in front of the other and gradually building assuredness as you go. Permission to trust yourself, granted.

Get Unstuck

1. TELL YOURSELF WHAT YOU NEED TO HEAR. Think about what you've been dying to hear from others (*You'd make an amazing manager!* or, *You're so good at creative projects.*) Don't wait for someone to say it to you, say it to yourself. Write it down on a sticky note and put it on your computer, mirror, or somewhere else you can readily see the reminder. Or, if you're unsure of yourself after giving a presentation to senior leaders, for example, spend five minutes noting reasons you're proud of yourself before turning to others for reassurance.

2. FREE YOURSELF TO TAKE ACTION. Make a list of everything you'd do if you gave yourself full permission to do exactly what you wanted. Think about areas where you've told yourself *I'm not ready yet* and write them down. Try asking yourself what would make this week, month, or year so awesome that it'd be worth popping a bottle of champagne. Some items on your *someday* or *maybe* list—like building your personal brand or speaking at a conference—may induce butterflies in your stomach, which is a good sign they are worth moving toward. Claiming your dreams and desires is the first step toward achieving them.

3. PUT PEOPLE'S PERCEPTIONS IN THEIR PLACE. Just because someone gives you advice or feedback doesn't mean you have to accept it. It's important to realize that other people's opinions about you are sometimes a projection of their insecurities, not a reflection of you. I love this trick from Brené Brown, who says, "I carry a small sheet of paper in my wallet that has written on it the names of people whose opinions of me matter. To be on that list, you have to love me for my strengths and struggles."

Strategy in Action: Travis

Through our coaching conversations, Travis realized he was overcomplicating things. He didn't need more input or knowledge. He already had everything he needed to start his business and simply needed to decide on his *very best next step* rather than trying to model pricing and revenue in the distant future. His first priority was to give himself permission to be successful and to free himself from the thought that people would perceive him as big-headed if he asked for business or introductions. I asked him to think, "What would this look like if it were easy and you already knew the exact right steps to take?"

As a result, he decided not to spend more time on the pricing matrix. Instead, he reached out to everyone who had asked him for advice during the past year to let them know he was available as a consultant for $100/hour—a rate he'd seen his hospital pay outside contractors. He had his first three clients within a month, and within six months, he was able to reevaluate and raise his prices when several clients asked for more complex service offerings. As part of the process of growing his business, Travis also allowed himself to experiment, play, and make mistakes. In order to reach beyond his network, Travis designed several introductory packages and created a video series about his methodology and approach. Even though few people saw the videos and only one client signed up for the new package, Travis used what he had learned to continue to refine his services and to be more articulate when describing his work process to potential clients. It was scary at first, but putting himself out there and slowly building his business through trial and error satisfied Travis's curiosity and creativity in a way that made him feel excited and proud. Solving clients' problems brought him joy and made him feel engaged. Through these small successes, Travis embraced a calmer and more optimistic attitude, which helped him see he had everything he needed to make his side gig a viable business.

Speak Up Shortcuts

How you talk to yourself matters, and imposter syndrome—feeling like you're incompetent, or a fake and a fraud—can be one of the biggest blockers to pursuing what's right for you. You can start changing your inner dialogue and how you speak to yourself this very minute.

IMPOSTER SYNDROME SOUNDS LIKE . . .		GIVING YOURSELF PERMISSION SOUNDS LIKE . . .
I have no idea what I'm doing.	→	I'll go for it and see what happens.
I need to do things correctly.	→	I can find a way that works for me.
I have to wait for the perfect timing.	→	I know I'll never be 100 percent ready, and I have to act anyway.
I have to make sure it's okay before proceeding.	→	I'll move ahead with my plan unless otherwise specified.
I'll look like I don't know what I'm doing.	→	I won't know everything, so it's wise to ask for help when I need it.
I have to work hard at all times to prove I'm good enough.	→	I value that the things that come easy to me are my strengths.
I always need to be doing more.	→	I can do less, but better.

YOUR PERMISSION SLIP

You may remember permission slips as licenses to move ahead or do something you wanted to do, like attend a field trip. As your next step in releasing the Honor Roll Hangover, I want you to write a permission slip to *yourself*. For your permission slip to matter, it has to come from *you*—not from me, your manager, or anyone else. In this way, you start to utilize your depth of thought, emotion, and self-awareness to make choices and rely on your own inner wisdom.

INSTRUCTIONS

1. *Bring to mind a situation that you're overthinking or overcomplicating.* It could also be an exciting opportunity that you've told yourself you're not cut out for.

2. *Fill out your permission slip.* I've included a template to guide you that covers the most common areas Sensitive Strivers struggle with.

3. *Keep it somewhere readily accessible.* I highly recommend hanging your permission slip on your wall or tucking it in your desk drawer so that you can pull it out whenever you need a reminder that you already have everything you need inside you to succeed (if you just get out of your own way).

4. *Revisit it as needed.* You'll revisit your permission slip later in this book, but you can also do this Exercise every month, every quarter, or whenever you find yourself up against a new challenge, risk, or leap that triggers doubt.

YOUR PERMISSION SLIP
Travis

I hereby grant myself complete and unlimited permission to <u>reach out to my network</u> in order to/for the purpose of <u>earning my first $100 as a consultant</u>.

Specifically:

I have permission to feel <u>nervous asking for introductions</u>.

I have permission to be <u>confident in the fact that I have a valuable skill to offer</u>.

I have permission to push when <u>I notice fear holding me back from offering my expertise</u>.

I have permission to rest when <u>I have a busy day at the hospital</u>.

I have permission to start <u>making a video series to promote my work</u>.

I have permission to try <u>sending emails to old coworkers, asking to grab coffee</u>.

I have permission to stop <u>worrying so much about the pricing matrix</u>.

I have permission to let go of <u>expecting myself to know everything about running a consulting firm</u>.

It's time to forgive myself for <u>spending a year trying to launch</u> and know that it helped <u>me sort out what's important from what's not</u>. I am ready to <u>put myself out there</u> and commit to <u>just starting</u> so that I can <u>hopefully secure my first consulting project within a month</u>.

Giving myself full permission and wholeheartedly believing in myself is important right now because <u>I'm ready for a new challenge</u>. I trust myself to <u>figure things out as I go</u> and know that no matter what happens, I've got this.

Sincerely,

<u>Travis</u>

YOUR PERMISSION SLIP

I hereby grant myself complete and unlimited permission to _____
_____ in order to/for the purpose of _____.
   Specifically:
I have permission to feel _____.
I have permission to be _____.
I have permission to push when _____.
I have permission to rest when _____.
I have permission to start _____.
I have permission to try _____.
I have permission to stop _____.
I have permission to let go _____.
   It's time to forgive myself for _____ and know
that it helped me _____. I am ready to _____
_____ and commit to _____ so that I can
_____.

   Giving myself full permission and wholeheartedly believing in myself is
important right now because _____. I trust myself to
_____ and know that no matter what happens, I've
got this.

   Sincerely,

   [Your Name]

PART II

TAME
SELF-SABOTAGE

4
Channel
Emotions
into an
Advantage

5
Overhaul
Your
Overthinking

6
Trust
Your
Gut

7
Build
Boundaries
Like a Boss

CHANNEL EMOTIONS
INTO AN ADVANTAGE

4

"Our feelings aren't the problem.
It's our relationship to them."

—AMBER RAE

DING. **AN EMAIL LANDED IN KATHERINE'S INBOX FROM** her boss, Beth. *Hey Kat, Mark just sent me the home page design. Let me know when you have time to discuss my comments.*

You've got to be joking, she thought to herself. *Doesn't he realize I'm his manager?* Katherine couldn't believe Mark had gone over her head and sent Beth the designs without running them past her first. She felt hot and dizzy as her anger set in, and she shut her eyes in an effort to collect herself.

Six months earlier, Katherine had been promoted to senior user interface designer, and only a month after that, she'd been tasked with supervising Mark, who was new to the company. Katherine's group was growing quickly, and she knew that learning to lead a team was one of the next steps on her career path, even though being a first-time manager made her nervous. Unfortunately, she hadn't been able to get into a rhythm with Mark, who had a very direct, dominant personality. He was extremely talented, but he was overly competitive and eager to take all the credit when the team did a good job. Sometimes Mark seemed frustrated with Katherine, and he had even ignored her instructions in meetings. With the website launch for a major client just a few weeks away, Katherine had made it clear that all designs needed her sign-off before heading to her boss, Beth, the creative director. Mark going over her head felt like a slap in the face.

Katherine could barely sit still as she tried to decide what to do. In a calm state of mind, the obvious answer would have been to address the situation with Mark directly, but Katherine's Emotionality was dialed up so high that she worried about her ability to respond without yelling—or crying. She was supposed to be in a position of authority, but she felt like a victim of her own emotions.

What was frustrating was that Katherine knew her emotions could sometimes be an asset. She had a keen ability to tune into how aspects of design—from the look and feel of the software to the actions users took—could evoke feelings of surprise and excitement. She had even won an industry award recognizing her achievements in Emotional Design for leading production on a project management software now used by Fortune 500 companies.

I'm overreacting, she thought. *Mark's the one who's out of line, not me.* Katherine decided to get back to Beth in a few hours, because for now, she needed to keep the launch on track. She clicked away from her inbox and back to the design she was working on, but she couldn't concentrate, and her body felt shaky and unsettled. "It took me three full hours to regain my composure," she told me later. "By the time I got my act together, the day was practically over." Like many of my clients, Katherine felt so overcome with emotion that she could neither handle the situation nor get anything else accomplished. Her Emotionality had gotten the better of her.

As Katherine discovered the hard way, trying to avoid your feelings is like trying to hold a beach ball underwater—at a certain point the ball forces its way to the surface no matter how hard you try to keep it from springing up. As long as you can hold the ball underwater, the surface of the pool is smooth and serene, but with only one hand free, your actions and energy are restricted. And when you loosen your grip, the ball inevitably comes rocketing to the surface anyway, making a big mess.

That's because avoiding emotions doesn't make them go away. Instead, Sensitive Strivers who struggle with unbalanced Emotionality spend an enormous amount of energy pretending that everything is okay while silently brooding and trying to process the intensity of their reactions. On the other end of the spectrum, letting your emotions run rampant can be similarly disruptive and exhausting if you live life constantly at the whim of an ever-changing stream of feelings. How then do you find balance between trying to ignore your emotions and letting them run the show? The answer is learning to accept your internal reactions and to manage them better. Feeling deeply and experiencing a range of emotions is the reality of who you are, and I'm here to tell you that leaning into and embracing that quality can be a competitive advantage—if you know how to do so effectively.

What You Resist Persists

Among my coaching clients, I'm known for saying, "What you resist persists," which means the longer you try to fight your emotions, change them, or tell yourself you're wrong for having them, the longer you'll struggle. This is particularly true in the workplace, where you've probably been led to believe that you need to tamp down your Emotionality to be successful. A better approach is to see your feelings as a natural extension of your innate strengths.

Just like the weather, emotions are always present whether we like it or not. They are important to identify, consider, and understand; however, they don't necessarily need to be an overriding factor in your plans. When the weather is bad (or not to your liking), it doesn't mean you deny it, focus all your attention on it, or cancel your plans because of it. What you do is accept the weather and adjust accordingly. So although it may seem easier said than done, you can begin treating your emotional life like you treat the weather—by accepting and preparing for it.

According to research, sensitive people tend to be more ashamed of their feelings and to believe that there's nothing they can do about them.

One of the most important things you can do for yourself is to see your emotions as a constant part of your inner life and to navigate them as they arise. Willingly allowing, acknowledging, and absorbing your feelings helps you to:

- **Avoid depletion.** High-intensity emotions like anxiety, distress, and nervousness are mentally taxing because they activate the body's fight-or-flight response. Emma Seppälä, author of *The Happiness Track*, notes that when sustained over long periods, high-intensity emotions can compromise your immune system, memory, and attention span. Even if you avoid them, high-intensity emotions don't go away. Paradoxically, they amplify, which only drains you further. Experiencing your emotions as they are—annoying, maybe, but not permanent—is much less of an energetic drag than pushing them away.

- **Influence your reactions.** In the throes of avoidance, you feel helpless and emotionally hijacked, as if you're spiraling out of control. When you accept your emotions, on the other hand, you have a chance to learn about your inner life and become more skilled at navigating it. You prove to yourself that you can handle your emotions flexibly, for example, by changing their intensity or duration and recovering more quickly.

- **Heed their message.** Emotions are a source of sensory intelligence and insight that give you important information about your needs or actions you can take to respond more authentically. Even so-called *bad* or negative emotions have a function. For instance, fear is one way to keep yourself safe and protected, and guilt signals the need to make amends. When you start thinking of your emotions as messengers, your relationship to them changes.

- **Strengthen your emotional balance.** Acceptance is different from passive resignation in that it involves dropping the struggle with your emotions *without* giving up on yourself. Ironically, accepting your emotions can boost your psychological health, contributing to fewer mood swings and higher overall life satisfaction. Most importantly, acceptance paves the way for you to leverage the upsides of your Emotionality rather than seeing it as something to be overcome.

YOUR EMOTIONS ARE A COMPETITIVE ADVANTAGE

Your STRIVE quality of Emotionality, once balanced, can serve you in many ways. Consider these facts:

- 90 percent of top performers are also high in emotional intelligence.

- 92 percent of executives rate soft skills like the ability to manage emotions as a critical priority in today's business environment, according to research from BetterUp.

- Teams with emotional leaders have greater trust, perform better, and innovate more.

- 75 percent of hiring managers said they would be more likely to promote an employee who is emotionally in touch.

- Because they are more attuned to their inner workings, emotional employees are good at motivating themselves, which reduces procrastination and boosts self-confidence and achievement of long-term goals.

Strategy: Find Your Center

No matter how intense the feeling, you can take charge of your emotional reactions before they take charge of you. Since all emotions start as energy in the body, calming your physiology is the quickest, surest way to become more present and in command of your experiences and yourself. Once you're centered, you can make sense of your responses and hear the messages your emotions are trying to send you.

Your nervous system is designed to go through regular cycles of charge and discharge, stimulation and relaxation. The problem is that many Sensitive Strivers are chronically overstimulated, which can make your Emotionality feel uncontrollable. When your sympathetic nervous system ramps up, you feel overwhelmed because the intensity of your response outpaces your capacity to process it. Stress hormones are released and your blood pressure and heart rate increase as your body prepares to fight or flee. That's exactly why the solution is to learn internal tools to manage your physiological response and to relax your nervous system before tackling anything else.

One simple way to get back to center is with a mindfulness technique called grounding. Grounding activates your parasympathetic nervous system, which is responsible for rest and recovery. When your parasympathetic nervous system switches on, your heart rate slows and blood flows to your prefrontal cortex, which improves your decision-making and concentration. Grounding directly impacts nerves in your brain's arousal center and signals to your mind and body that it's safe to settle down. There are dozens of different grounding exercises you can try, everything from deep breathing and progressive relaxation to visualization. Most are inconspicuous, meaning you can do them on a call, at your desk, or even while driving. Below are a few of my favorites, and in the upcoming Exercise in this chapter, you'll be guided to discover which works best for you.

The 5-4-3-2-1 Tool. Select five things you see around you (a white notepad or a spot on the ceiling, for example). Describe to yourself in detail the things you see, either out loud or silently. Pick four things you can touch or feel, such as your tongue in your mouth or your hands in your lap. Notice the texture, temperature, and sensations you're experiencing. Pick three things you hear (like a phone ringing or the hum of an air conditioner). Say two things you can smell (if you can't smell anything, name your two favorite scents). Name one thing you can taste (like a lingering toothpaste taste). Engaging all five senses helps bring your attention back to the present moment.

Clench and Release. Visualize yourself gathering all your uncomfortable emotions up into your palms. Make a tight fist for five to ten seconds. Then let go and open your hands as if you were releasing the feelings and letting them melt away.

Box Breathing. Breathe in for four seconds. Hold air in your lungs for four seconds. Exhale for four seconds. Hold your breath, lungs emptied, for four seconds. Ideally, you'll repeat these steps for three to five minutes, but even one minute is enough to experience an effect. You can find guided visualizations online to assist you in a box breathing practice if you're just getting started.

Instead of finding yourself drained by high-intensity negative feelings like worry, fright, or humiliation, grounding helps you move toward low-intensity positive emotions like serenity, contentment, and tranquility so you feel alive, at peace, and in control. Best of all, you can process and sort through your feelings in an evenhanded way.

Once you're in a calmer, more composed state physically, you're in a better position to figure out how you want to move ahead. For most Sensitive Strivers, this is the biggest challenge of all because you may feel paralyzed by all the different options. Don't worry, because in future chapters you'll learn how to make decisions that are aligned with your boundaries, core values, and the preferences you have for your life and career. But for now, here are some questions to ask yourself:

- Do you have all the information you need to make a decision? If not, what can you do to get a better understanding?
- What would you regret not doing or saying?
- What's the worst that could reasonably happen if you choose a certain action? Are you okay with this outcome?
- What's the best that could happen if you choose a certain action? Are you satisfied with this outcome?

Get Unstuck

1. GET GRANULAR. You can't manage what you can't put into words, so define your emotions with specificity. For example, when clients tell me they feel overwhelmed by changing priorities at work, we explore it more. Do they feel disappointment because they think they're unable to deliver results? Or embarrassment because they're concerned they're letting their teams down? Studies show that naming your emotions immediately releases their grip over you.

2. CREATE DISTANCE. Gain objectivity by writing about your emotions. Try using the structure, *I'm having the feeling that I'm* [emotion] *because . . .* For example: *I'm having the feeling that I'm demoralized because I have so much on my plate and not enough time to accomplish it all.* Saying *I'm having the feeling that* helps you create distance from your feelings and trust that they are temporary inner experiences.

3. CHANGE YOUR ENVIRONMENT. Physically disconnecting from the situation always helps. Step away from your desk to take a walk, do a quick meditation from your couch, or simply get up to grab a cup of coffee.

4. DRAW ON YOUR HEROES. Imagine how a person you admire might respond to an emotionally overwhelming situation like being interrupted during a meeting or getting denied a raise, for example. What would they do? This fresh insight can guide how you react.

5. LEARN YOUR TRIGGERS. Pay attention to the circumstances and people present when your Emotionality becomes unbalanced so that you can better anticipate and manage your reactions in the future. For instance, if you know being rushed sends you into panic, mitigate time crunches such as extending your team one-on-ones from thirty to forty-five minutes.

Strategy in Action: Katherine

As the office emptied out for the day, Katherine read Beth's email over and over again. She couldn't possibly respond productively or make a good decision about what to do while in an upset headspace, so first, she closed her laptop and took a moment to concentrate on her body. Her shoulders hurt, and she could feel that she had probably spent the day with them hunched toward her ears. Knowing this was one of her common stress responses, she accepted that this was something she had to address now. Instead of wishing her feelings away or ignoring them, she practiced box breathing at her desk and immediately felt her body relax. On a notepad, she journaled in response to the sentence structure *I'm having the feeling that* . . . Getting her thoughts out was not only cathartic, but she could sense her muscle tension melt away as a result.

With her body calm and her mind clear, Katherine set up a meeting with Beth first thing in the morning. She was still angry, but she also knew that she needed Mark and the high-quality work product he produced to keep the project on schedule. Katherine decided that she would have to wait until the website was launched to directly address the situation. She and Beth reviewed the design together the next day and sent comments to Mark via team chat. When Beth realized that Katherine had not seen the designs until that minute, she sighed, and Katherine said, "I know this is a problem, and I'm going to deal with it after the launch."

"I know you can handle it, but in the meantime, I'll say something," Beth said. She tagged a note onto the end of her feedback letting Mark know that she expected him to go to Katherine first before sending her anything else going forward.

Katherine was relieved that the issue was resolved in the short term and that Beth hadn't been nearly as frustrated with her as she had feared. In our next session, we began to talk about how to deal with Mark in the future. We'll return to Katherine later in the book in Chapter Eight when we talk about core values and in Chapter Twelve in our discussion on assertive communication to see how she tackled the issue with Mark.

SELF-CARE VERSUS SELF-SABOTAGE

It's impossible to talk about emotional well-being without talking about self-care. Self-care is important and essential, but just because something feels good doesn't mean it's helping. When caring for yourself is fueled by the desire for distraction or avoidance, you may escape through shopping or snacks, or think *I deserve it* to justify having a bottle of wine after a rough day. Real self-care is about rewarding habits that sustain instead of drain you.

- **PHYSICAL SELF-CARE:** Physical self-care can include exercise, eating well, hydrating, taking a sick day when you don't feel well, and getting enough sleep.

- **EMOTIONAL SELF-CARE:** Beyond identifying and accepting your feelings, emotional self-care also includes setting boundaries and saying no.

- **SPIRITUAL SELF-CARE:** This can mean religion, but it more broadly encompasses any ritual or practice that connects you to your higher self or the Universe, like meditation, time in nature, and journaling.

- **INTELLECTUAL SELF-CARE:** You can nourish your mind by choosing a documentary over a reality TV show or playing a board game with your partner at the end of a hard day instead of venting about work. Recently, one of my clients said to me that self-promotion at work is an act of self-care. I had to agree.

- **SOCIAL SELF-CARE:** Grabbing dinner with a friend, sending your mom a card, or getting support from an online community are all ways to build strong, respectful relationships.

- **SAFETY AND SECURITY SELF-CARE:** Taking care of your finances and planning your career path fall under this category.

The next time you feel stressed-out or overwhelmed, check in. Is the amount of time and energy you've given to each category of self-care well balanced? Self-care is fluid, so it may look different depending on the day, your mood, and circumstances. Sometimes it looks like taking a few hours off to let your brain rest. On other days, it's pushing through a slump to prove to yourself what you're capable of.

CHOOSE-YOUR-OWN
GROUNDING ADVENTURE

In Part I of this book, you reflected and assessed. Now, in Part II, you'll experiment with new ways of approaching situations and yourself.

To Find Your Center, start by trying different grounding techniques to find one or two that are effective for you.

INSTRUCTIONS

1. *Find quiet time.* After work or on a weekend—whenever you have a short block of quiet, uninterrupted time—put aside ten or fifteen minutes to try the grounding techniques in this chapter. Each will take no more than a couple seconds to one or two minutes.

2. *Recall a recent example of a situation where your Emotionality was unbalanced.* If you rated yourself as unbalanced in this area in the Exercise in Chapter One, think of a situation that represents why you'd like to give this particular STRIVE quality attention. Maybe you felt ashamed that you weren't meeting expectations or felt disappointed that a project wasn't moving quickly enough. As unpleasant as it may be, bring yourself back to that moment and try grounding yourself.

3. *Pause after trying each technique.* Notice how your physical state has changed. Has your breathing slowed down? Have your thoughts shifted? It's likely you feel more clearheaded. Use the table provided to note your experience. Aim for subtle shifts to start. Don't get discouraged if you feel awkward. You're rewiring your brain, which can feel weird at first.

4. *Pick one grounding technique that resonates with you.* Commit to using it consistently. The key is to practice regularly and in low-stakes situations, so that your preferred technique kicks in when you feel emotionally provoked.

5. *Create a cue.* Remind yourself that you have your grounding technique at your disposal. You could put a sticky note on your lunch bag or use a calendar notification that comes up at the start of your work day.

CHOOSE-YOUR-OWN
GROUNDING ADVENTURE
Katherine

GROUNDING TECHNIQUE	MY OBSERVATIONS
The 5-4-3-2-1 Tool	This one didn't do it for me. My mind started wandering, and I began to worry about deadlines.
Clench and Release	I'm a very visual person, so I liked the idea of imagining that I was releasing my anger and annoyance. I felt my shoulders relax after I let go of my fists.
Box Breathing	Wow, what a difference box breathing made! I could feel my heart rate slow down and it no longer felt like it was beating out my chest. Afterwards it was like a warm glow rushed over me.

The grounding technique I commit to trying is <u>Box Breathing</u>, *and I'll remind myself to practice it by* <u>drawing a square on a sticky note and placing it in my lunch bag so I see it as soon as I open it.</u>

CHOOSE-YOUR-OWN
GROUNDING ADVENTURE

_____

GROUNDING TECHNIQUE	MY OBSERVATIONS
The 5-4-3-2-1 Tool	
Clench and Release	
Box Breathing	

_The grounding technique I commit to trying is _____
and I'll remind myself to practice it by _____._

OVERHAUL YOUR OVERTHINKING

5

"Exchange your overthinking for overwhelming peace that says, I can be okay without knowing everything."

—MORGAN HARPER NICHOLS

WE ALL HAVE A NEAR-CONSTANT STREAM OF THOUGHTS running through our minds, especially during the workday when there are so many decisions to make and dynamics to weigh. But overthinking, or the tendency to get trapped in your own head, happens when your Thoughtfulness and Vigilance go into overdrive, which can leave you stuck in negative mental loops that waste valuable time and energy.

Overthinking takes many forms, and the stories you tell yourself may not reflect the truth of the matter. Just like the check engine light on your car, overthinking calls attention to the fact that your STRIVE qualities need recalibration. As you integrate the practices from this book into your life, it will become second nature to make these kinds of adjustments, but at the beginning, you'll probably need to stop and actively shift your mindset like Cassie, the client in my next story, when she got the opportunity to level up.

"How was your day? How's the keynote prep going?" Cassie's wife asked as she peeked her head out of their kitchen into the entryway. "I can't do it," Cassie huffed. "I'm going to tell Greg that I changed my mind, and he'll have to present at the conference instead of me."

A week earlier, Cassie's manager Greg had asked her to represent the company at the biggest human resources event of the year, where she would deliver a talk about how they had used technology to implement equitable hiring practices. When Greg had initially proposed the idea, Cassie had eagerly agreed—this opportunity would expose her to senior leaders and position her as a rising star among her peers—but now she found herself flip-flopping on her decision to go to the conference at all. Cassie was four years into a career switch, and she couldn't help but imagine all the ways her performance might fall short. She walked into the kitchen and sat down at the table. "A few weeks ago Greg said I could benefit from becoming a more concise communicator," she said, her eyes cast down. "If I get up in front of a group this big and important, everyone will see that I clearly have no idea what I'm doing."

"Oh, come on!" her wife exclaimed. "How many times has Greg said you're the best presenter he has? I was there when he said so at the company party last year. And besides, the software implementation was all your idea. Please, Cassie, don't let one tiny piece of feedback hold you back."

After college, Cassie spent several years as a grade school teacher, but due to budget cuts, she had been laid off four years before. Although she considered going back to graduate school in education, she decided that a career in human resources might offer more fulfillment and job security. Cassie considered herself a lifelong learner who was always hungry to grow and improve, so she had no qualms about working on her human resources degree during nights and weekends while she did temp work to pay her bills. She had even enrolled in a certificate program to improve her skill set. Cassie's ambition paired with her training made her an attractive hire, so much so that she beat out two other candidates for a role as Human Resources Associate at a financial services company. Within her first year on the job, she had been promoted to manager.

The role was everything she had hoped for. She built a good relationship with Greg, who was supportive and saw further growth opportunities for her at the company. Cassie also enjoyed her coworkers, who were kind, collaborative, and fun to be around—the workplace environment of her dreams. She adored popping on her headphones first thing in the morning and plugging away on recruiting tasks until lunchtime. It was during one of these moments that Cassie first thought of using software to remove unconscious bias in the company's hiring processes. As a teacher, Cassie had been involved in technology-driven diversity and inclusion initiatives within the school system, and she saw a similar opportunity within her new company to bring in higher-quality candidates from a bigger pool. Greg had tasked her with implementing the project and rolling it out to staff, and it had been so successful that there was talk of another promotion and a pay raise in the next performance cycle.

On good days, Cassie felt she was finally on the right path and that she had a lot to offer. On other days, her confidence wavered, and she found herself mentally whirling in circles to the soundtrack of an inner critic shouting that she didn't know what she was doing. She frequently credited her progress to BS-ing her way through projects and making it up as she went along—never factoring in her aptitude, her work ethic, and her willingness to learn on the job. And when Greg recognized her contributions in meetings, Cassie laughed off his praise and described her successes as flukes. She often found herself tossing and turning at night, worried about being let go again. Now, as she imagined standing up on stage and speaking about her work, she defaulted to the worst-case scenario. "Everyone will know I'm a phony! I don't think I can do it," Cassie said as they sat down to dinner. "Don't say no yet," her wife encouraged her. "Give yourself a few days and see how you feel then." Cassie was skeptical that more time would help. Even though she knew she would regret giving up the opportunity, she just couldn't put the brakes on her unproductive deliberation and evaluation. As hard as she tried, she couldn't stop overthinking.

The Many Faces of Overthinking

Overthinking comes in a few forms. It can include:

Rumination. When you're ruminating, you're dwelling and living in the past. You analyze and replay situations over and over. You may rehash conversations, dissect people's body language, and stress about what you did or didn't say. Inventing what-if scenarios (*What if I had spoken up? What if I had taken that job? What if I had reached out to my mentor earlier?*) is also common.

Future tripping. You may find yourself worrying about the future at the expense of enjoying the present. For example, you may think, *I'm going to embarrass myself tomorrow when I give that presentation and forget everything I'm supposed to say*, or maybe you find yourself preoccupied and distracted by upcoming deadlines when you're hanging out with your family.

Imposter syndrome. Imposter syndrome is the sneaking suspicion that you're a fake or fraud, despite evidence that you are competent and accomplished. You may doubt your capabilities, undermine your expertise, and attribute your success to luck. *If I can do it, anyone can* and *I give the impression that I'm smarter than I really am* are just a few examples of thoughts related to imposter syndrome.

Indecision. You can see many sides of a situation, but struggle to choose between multiple courses of action because you fear making a mistake or want to maximize your choices. You may second-guess your weekend plans or experience analysis paralysis (excessively researching or overanalyzing), which stalls action. Hesitation or going back on commitments in order to please someone else often accompany indecisiveness.

Strategy: Name It and Reframe It

Overthinking is driven by negative self-talk, which in psychology is more well known as cognitive distortions. Cognitive distortions are difficult to recognize because they can be a lot like white noise—you get so used to hearing them that you don't even realize they're operating in the background—but they are. Cognitive distortions are:

- Automatic, self-critical thought patterns that drive all forms of overthinking
- Inaccurate, based on assumptions, and unknowingly cause distress
- A reflection of fear coming through versus your intuition nudging you

The most effective strategy to transform the unhelpful thoughts that come along with overthinking is naming and reframing. Naming your unhelpful thoughts and then reframing them helps improve your perspective and point you toward more constructive ways to interpret events, so that you can see new possibilities and find solutions instead of hitting mental dead ends. The goal of reframing isn't to always have perfectly balanced thoughts (because you won't), but rather to slow down, and take in the bigger picture. You're not changing your thoughts from negative to positive with brute force. Instead, you're gently reminding your brain to be fair, open, and curious versus critical and judgmental.

There are many different types of cognitive distortions, but here are the most common ones that affect Sensitive Strivers and how to think about reframing them. The Exercise in this chapter will help you target and neutralize cognitive distortions, so you'll be ready to tune into your intuition next in Chapter Six.

ALL-OR-NOTHING THINKING

You: See situations and yourself in terms of absolutes, without room for middle ground.

Sounds like: *If I don't get this right, I'm a complete failure.*

Reframe by: Look for nuance in situations. When your mind presents only two forks in the road, pause and ask if you might be missing some options. Specifically, it helps to swap out *or* or *but* for *and*.

Sounds like: *I had some wonderful wins this week* and *some setbacks that were difficult.*

OVERGENERALIZATION

You: Take one unfavorable instance and generalize it to an ongoing pattern.

Sounds like: *I'm always screwing up.*

Reframe by: Stop using extreme words like *always*, *never*, *all*, and *every*. Treat events in isolation. Just because something happened once doesn't mean it will happen again.

Sounds like: *This presentation wasn't my best. I'll be more prepared for the next one.*

FILTERING

You: Ignore all the positive aspects of a situation and focus on the negative aspects only.

Sounds like: *I'm devastated by the flaw my boss pointed out even though the rest of her feedback was good.*

Reframe by: Do a quick cost-benefit analysis and ask yourself, *How will it help me to keep focusing on the bad, and how will it hurt me?* If focusing on the negatives is clearly doing more harm, you may find it easier to let go and move on.

Sounds like: *I'm glad my boss acknowledged my ability to execute, and I'll work on my strategic thinking skills.*

CATASTROPHIZING

You: Expect the worst.

Sounds like: *I'm going to get fired and end up broke and homeless.*

Reframe by: Take a moment to acknowledge what is going well in the present moment. Then tackle your fears head-on. What is the worst that could actually happen and how would you deal with it? When you explore the idea to its extreme, you'll find you can create a plan for almost anything life throws at you.

Sounds like: *It's unlikely I'll get fired, but even if I do, I'd get my resume out there and start contacting my network.*

DISQUALIFYING THE POSITIVE

You: Reject positive attributes about yourself, such as compliments and achievements.

Sounds like: *Anyone could have done it.*

Reframe by: When a *yes, but . . .* rationalization enters your mind, counter it by focusing on indisputable attributes about yourself.

Sounds like: *I have a lot to offer, and other people recognize it even if I sometimes am slow to see it myself.*

JUMPING TO CONCLUSIONS

You: Make unwarranted judgments and convince yourself you know what other people are feeling and thinking without their saying so.

Sounds like: *He didn't respond to my email. I know he hates me.*

Reframe by: Brainstorm five other possible explanations or ways of viewing the situation (you can count them off on your hand). Question how often your fear-based predictions are on-point and figure out what you can do to test your assumptions.

Sounds like: *He didn't respond to my email, which means he might be busy. I'll follow up with him to see how he's doing and not take it personally.*

EMOTIONAL REASONING

You: Experience a difficult emotion and make it mean something bad about yourself.

Sounds like: *I feel sad, so I must be a bore to be around.*

Reframe by: Describe the facts of the situation, rather than your emotional response to them, and try to separate yourself from your emotions so that you can see them more objectively. Remember that even a negative emotion can lead to a positive outcome like rethinking a situation or setting a boundary.

Sounds like: *I feel down because I'm behind at work. This is a chance for me to reassess what's important and deprioritize what's not.*

SHOULD STATEMENTS

You: Attach yourself to a certain outcome or expectation about how things should be.

Sounds like: *I should be better at this by now.*

Reframe by: Question whose expectations you're trying to live up to. Is it the voice of a parent? A mentor? Your boss? Even though you may be walking around with a set of rules and standards you live by, consider who made these rules and if they allow you to live the kind of purposeful life you want to live.

Sounds like: *I'm not an expert yet, though I'm improving each week.*

PERSONALIZATION

You: Hold yourself accountable for things that are beyond your control and assume responsibility for the happiness of those around you.

Sounds like: *The project failed because I didn't spend enough time on it.*

Reframe by: Be gentle with yourself when you make mistakes. Self-criticism doesn't motivate, self-compassion does. List what is truly within your control and what isn't.

Sounds like: *I can be more disciplined about how I spend my time, but I must keep in mind that there will be aspects of any project that are out of my control.*

DOUBLE STANDARD

You: Hold yourself to a higher standard than everyone else.

Sounds like: *I have to respond to our client within an hour—even on weekends—but the rest of the team can take their time.*

Reframe by: Drop perfectionism, and treat yourself with the respect and consideration you give others.

Sounds like: *I'm the one putting pressure on myself to respond immediately. I'll honor my need for recovery time and punt calls to Monday.*

Get Unstuck

1. REMIND YOURSELF WITH A RUBBER BAND. Keep a rubber band or hair tie on your wrist. Each time you notice that you're overthinking, snap the band and silently say *STOP*. This brings you back to the present moment, and out of rumination or future tripping.

2. PERSONIFY YOUR INNER CRITIC. Try giving your inner critic a harmless name. I had a client who called hers Bart, which seems a lot less threatening than the elusive inner critic. Another client bought a lovable-looking monster figurine from a dollar store and placed it on her desk. It was a helpful totem that helped her realize her inner critic wasn't as big and scary as she made it out to be in her head.

3. LET YOUR THOUGHTS FLOAT AWAY. Picture each unhelpful thought as a balloon. Imagine yourself releasing the string and watch as it floats into the air, out of sight.

4. PLAY WITH THEM. I like to sing my self-critical thoughts to the tune of Belinda Carlisle's "Heaven Is a Place on Earth" or Hanson's "MMMBop." You can also bring humor and lightness to your thoughts by changing the typeface. In your mind's eye, picture making the font of your thoughts teeny tiny Comic Sans, for example. You'll find it's much easier to approach your thinking lightly.

Strategy in Action: Cassie

For the rest of the week, Cassie woke up in a cold sweat after nightmares about potentially flubbing the keynote. On the one hand, she wanted to represent her company—she loved her job, and she was proud of the work she had done—but she worried that a lackluster performance would prove she was actually incompetent and that she would eventually be laid off again.

Luckily, we had a coaching session the day before she was scheduled to touch base with Greg. Cassie and I had already been working together for half a year, and we had spent most of that time working through the Strategies and Exercises in this book to help her get a grip on her fears, realizing that no matter how strong they became, they couldn't hurt her. When she and I talked, we discussed the fact that her Thoughtfulness, which was frequently a strength, was working against her as she tried to make this decision. I pointed out that she was disqualifying the positive, choosing to focus on Greg's one piece of constructive feedback and not on her achievements and progress over the last two years in the new role. As we unpacked what was underlying her indecision surrounding the keynote, Cassie began to zero in on the persistent thoughts that drove her imposter syndrome. Whenever she was nervous about a new challenge, she also found herself slipping into overgeneralization, thinking, *I'm going to screw this up, just like I do with every job.* Naming this thought helped Cassie admit that the layoff several years back had shaken her confidence and that even though Greg had said she could be more concise, it was an isolated comment and also something she could work on and improve.

Since we didn't have a lot of time until she needed to either tell Greg she had changed her mind or start writing the keynote, I walked Cassie through the thought tracking exercise you'll learn next. It involved having her repeat back to me what went through her head as she was weighing the decision to step down from or up to the speaking opportunity. During our session, we wrote down examples of her personal brand of negative self-talk and I assisted her with mapping those to cognitive distortions.

We worked through one of her persistent, negative thoughts together—the idea that she had to perform flawlessly or else everyone would know she was a fraud, which was an example of all-or-nothing thinking. Then, we looked at the evidence to support or to refute that thought. Yes, it was true she was still fairly new and needed to prove herself if she wanted to level up, and yes, this was a big opportunity with exposure to influential people. But, the counterevidence was also true. Greg had called Cassie his best presenter. She thought back over the past two years and could clearly see that she had become more skilled at presenting to groups because her job required giving employee trainings. Though giving a keynote was different than presenting to a small group, she knew she could translate her skills from one environment to another. Finally, we focused on her sense of accomplishment and belonging at her company, and she admitted that the hiring initiative, which had been an enormous success, was something *she* had brought to the company through her unique combination of expertise and insight.

That night before bed, Cassie pulled out the permission slip she had written six months before and reread it. In addition to giving herself permission to see through the diversity hiring initiative, Cassie had also given herself permission to succeed even though her teaching career hadn't gone as she had hoped. In the morning, Cassie decided to go through with the keynote and scheduled a meeting in two weeks to review her first draft with Greg. Naturally, she had a mix of thoughts about the situation, but naming and reframing allowed her to muster her courage to move forward. We'll see Cassie again in Chapter Thirteen when we tackle rebounding from setbacks, but that night Cassie and her wife celebrated with a glass of wine, and Cassie slept well knowing that she had short-circuited her overthinking and had made a decision that allowed her to use her STRIVE qualities to advance rather than sabotage the goals she had for herself.

BALANCE YOUR THOUGHTS

Overthinking can feel like an impossible problem. Keeping a thought journal changes that by making cognitive distortions visible to you. Five minutes a day is all you need to start. Soon it will become more natural to approach situations and yourself with greater equanimity and self-compassion.

INSTRUCTIONS

1. *Describe the situation.* What led to the overthinking: Where were you? When was it? Who was involved?

2. *Write down the negative thought.* Don't worry about phrasing things perfectly. It's enough to say *I don't know for sure what I'm thinking, but I wonder if it has something to do with* _____.

3. *Choose the cognitive distortion it represents.* The most common tend to be all-or-nothing thinking, filtering, and jumping to conclusions.

4. *List supporting evidence as to why the thought might be true.* Stick with verifiable data, not opinions and interpretations. An opinion sounds like, *I'm horrible at my job.* A fact sounds like, *I made a typo in the email.*

5. *List nonsupporting evidence.* Are there experiences (no matter how minor) that contradict this thought or indicate it's not completely true all of the time?

6. *Highlight the consequences.* Consider the physical, psychological, and professional downsides.

7. *Create a more balanced thought.* Aim for statements that are rooted in reality. The more uplifting and encouraging, the better. Use these questions to help you:

    • How might someone who is confident respond?
    • How would I advise my best friend to approach this?
    • What thought helps me feel energized and powerful?
    • What would I believe if I knew everything was going to work out?

8. *Note down other observations.* How does your more balanced thought make you feel? You may not go from fearful to elated in one sitting, but going from frustrated to at ease can be a breakthrough.

BALANCE YOUR THOUGHTS

Cassie

DATE	August 21st

SITUATION

Worrying about bombing the keynote, recounting every time I had ever rambled in a meeting.

NEGATIVE THOUGHT

I'm clearly a weak communicator.

SUPPORTING EVIDENCE

About a month ago Greg gave me feedback saying I needed to work on concise communication.

CONSEQUENCES

- ○ Waste time overthinking
- ○ Avoid a task
- ○ Overfunction by "saving" others
- ✗ Beat myself up
- ✗ Drain my motivation
- ○ Decline an opportunity
- ○ Work too much
- ○ Other

_____

_____

EXAMPLE OF

- ○ All-or-nothing thinking
- ○ Overgeneralization
- ○ Filtering
- ○ Catastrophizing
- ✗ Disqualifying the positive
- ○ Jumping to conclusions
- ○ Emotional reasoning
- ○ Should statements
- ○ Personalization
- ○ Double standard

NONSUPPORTING EVIDENCE

My positive performance reviews, the fact that I'm in line for a promotion and was invited to give this keynote—all of that is evidence I can speak and present well.

MORE BALANCED THOUGHT

- ○ I can focus on the bigger picture.
- ○ I'm only human, and I can give myself slack.
- ○ I choose to take this situation at face value.
- ○ There's a lesson to take away from this.
- ○ I could interpret this differently.
- ✗ I know I can handle this.
- ○ This outcome actually serves me.

My balanced thought:

   I'm a solid communicator and I'm

   motivated to keep improving.

COMMENTS AND OTHER OBSERVATIONS

It's awkward at first to take in and acknowledge the praise I've been given. I notice this is a pattern I have at home, too, with my wife, which affects our marriage.

BALANCE YOUR THOUGHTS
Cassie

DATE	August 21st

SITUATION
Sick to my stomach that I'll be unable to answer audience questions, exposed as incompetent, fired.

NEGATIVE THOUGHT
I'm going to screw this up, just like I do with every job.

SUPPORTING EVIDENCE
I was laid off from teaching.

CONSEQUENCES
- ☒ Waste time overthinking
- ○ Avoid a task
- ○ Overfunction by "saving" others
- ○ Beat myself up
- ○ Drain my motivation
- ○ Decline an opportunity
- ○ Work too much
- ○ Other
  _____
  _____

EXAMPLE OF
- ○ All-or-nothing thinking
- ☒ Overgeneralization
- ○ Filtering
- ○ Catastrophizing
- ○ Disqualifying the positive
- ○ Jumping to conclusions
- ○ Emotional reasoning
- ○ Should statements
- ○ Personalization
- ○ Double standard

NONSUPPORTING EVIDENCE
I've been promoted several times in the last four years.

MORE BALANCED THOUGHT
- ○ I can focus on the bigger picture.
- ○ I'm only human, and I can give myself slack.
- ○ I choose to take this situation at face value.
- ○ There's a lesson to take away from this.
- ○ I could interpret this differently.
- ○ I know I can handle this.
- ☒ This outcome actually serves me.

My balanced thought:
Being laid off as a teacher was the catalyst that launched my HR career.

COMMENTS AND OTHER OBSERVATIONS
I didn't realize—and it's eye-opening to see—how much this negative script was operating in the background and affecting how I approached my work and myself.

BALANCE YOUR THOUGHTS
Cassie

DATE	August 22nd

SITUATION

In my coaching session with Melody, talking about whether or not I should go forward with the keynote.

NEGATIVE THOUGHT

I have to perform flawlessly or else the event is a failure. And I'm a failure.

SUPPORTING EVIDENCE

There's a lot riding on the keynote in terms of the company's reputation in the industry.

CONSEQUENCES

- ○ Waste time overthinking
- ○ Avoid a task
- ○ Overfunction by "saving" others
- ○ Beat myself up
- ○ Drain my motivation
- ☒ Decline an opportunity
- ○ Work too much
- ○ Other

_____

_____

EXAMPLE OF

- ☒ All-or-nothing thinking
- ○ Overgeneralization
- ○ Filtering
- ○ Catastrophizing
- ○ Disqualifying the positive
- ○ Jumping to conclusions
- ○ Emotional reasoning
- ○ Should statements
- ○ Personalization
- ○ Double standard

NONSUPPORTING EVIDENCE

Even if there are a few hiccups in my presentation, it won't be the end of the world.

MORE BALANCED THOUGHT

- ○ I can focus on the bigger picture.
- ☒ I'm only human, and I can give myself slack.
- ○ I choose to take this situation at face value.
- ○ There's a lesson to take away from this.
- ○ I could interpret this differently.
- ○ I know I can handle this.
- ○ This outcome actually serves me.

My balanced thought:

The middle ground is preparing to the best of my ability and showing up 100 percent.

COMMENTS AND OTHER OBSERVATIONS

I feel relief having worked through the thought, although I am still nervous (in a good way!).

BALANCE YOUR THOUGHTS

DATE	

SITUATION

NEGATIVE THOUGHT

SUPPORTING EVIDENCE

CONSEQUENCES

- ◯ Waste time overthinking
- ◯ Avoid a task
- ◯ Overfunction by "saving" others
- ◯ Beat myself up
- ◯ Drain my motivation
- ◯ Decline an opportunity
- ◯ Work too much
- ◯ Other

_____

_____

EXAMPLE OF

- ◯ All-or-nothing thinking
- ◯ Overgeneralization
- ◯ Filtering
- ◯ Catastrophizing
- ◯ Disqualifying the positive
- ◯ Jumping to conclusions
- ◯ Emotional reasoning
- ◯ Should statements
- ◯ Personalization
- ◯ Double standard

NONSUPPORTING EVIDENCE

MORE BALANCED THOUGHT

- ◯ I can focus on the bigger picture.
- ◯ I'm only human, and I can give myself slack.
- ◯ I choose to take this situation at face value.
- ◯ There's a lesson to take away from this.
- ◯ I could interpret this differently.
- ◯ I know I can handle this.
- ◯ This outcome actually serves me.

My balanced thought:

_____

_____

COMMENTS AND OTHER OBSERVATIONS

TRUST YOUR GUT

6

*"The intuitive mind is a sacred gift and
the rational mind is a faithful servant. We have
created a society that honors the servant and
has forgotten the gift."*

—ALBERT EINSTEIN

ABOUT A YEAR AFTER STARTING HIS CONSULTING PRACTICE, Travis, who you met in Chapter Three, told me that he felt as if he was at a crossroads. His business had been so successful, he wondered whether he should take a risk and go all-in on his startup or commit to his full-time job at the hospital. He was earning several thousand dollars a month and had a waiting list of clients, but he often found himself working on weekends when he used to spend time running and going out with his partner and their friends. One part of him felt excited by the idea of taking the leap from traditional employment to entrepreneurship. Another part cautioned against leaving. From a practical standpoint, he'd be giving up great health insurance and a steady paycheck. Travis also really enjoyed his day-to-day responsibilities, his team, and knowing that their work was critical to saving patients' lives and keeping the hospital humming.

Travis was learning a lot as a consultant even though his fear of disappointing clients had led him to take on too many projects simultaneously. The steady stream of inquiries had convinced him that his services were in demand, but as a cautious Sensitive Striver, he wanted to avoid making a decision he would regret. His Sensitivity to many different inputs was part of why he was so good at the technical details of his job, but right now, it was making him feel more confused and lost. The one thing he knew was that his "pause and check" system, as researcher Elaine Aron calls it, was flashing, cautioning him to slow down before entering a potentially risky situation. While this tendency had benefited him in the past (stopping him from blurting out uninformed thoughts at meetings and from drinking too much at company events and embarrassing himself, for example), right now, his heightened inhibition was simply keeping him stuck. Travis had spent many coffee-fueled late nights going through every rational exercise he could think of to try and reach a decision—creating a pro/con list, doing a SWOT (strengths, weaknesses, opportunities, or threats) analysis, and even running projected income numbers for the next five years, but he still wasn't any closer to knowing what to do. Instead, he felt strung out and unsettled.

It didn't help that every time Travis checked social media, he was bombarded with messages pushing him to grow his business, from ads that pitched coaching programs in how to scale a side business to one million to updates from colleagues celebrating a venture capital raise for their own companies. The obligation he felt to become a consulting rock star weighed heavy on him and ran counter to why he had started a business, which was to diversify his income and make full use of his skills. In the back of his mind, Travis knew he didn't want to end up like his father, who had stayed in a job with a pension even though he had always talked about starting a business, but Travis didn't know how to use that information to become happier and more fulfilled. By the time we sat down together, Travis was overwhelmed by the pressure and the noise of analyzing the situation. He had done the math and considered his choices from all angles, but the one thing he hadn't done was tune into his intuition.

Despite popular belief, intuition isn't some woo-woo, spiritual concept. There's a deep neurological basis for it, and your gut instincts can offer tremendous value. The problem is that most Sensitive Strivers spend years actively thwarting their intuition, favoring the voices of other people over their own. You may have already experienced the effects of making decisions that way. Perhaps you drove yourself to exhaustion or illness even though your gut said to take a rest. Or maybe you kept quiet rather than speak up and risk the possibility of embarrassment when you had a new and different idea. All of it may have left you with the symptoms of an Honor Roll Hangover. If you look back at your Wheel of Balance from Chapter One, those feelings are likely reflected there. In the first half of Part II, we've talked about recognizing and reconnecting to how you think and feel so that your life can be a reflection of what you both need and want. Then, once you've found your center, and peeled back the layers of your negative self-talk, your intuition will be there to guide you to your true nature.

Your Sensitive Striver Sixth Sense

You may know intuition by another name—hunch, gut feeling, deeper knowing. It's the ability to immediately understand something without conscious reasoning. In other words, answers and solutions come to you, but you may not be aware why or how. Psychologically speaking, intuition works on implicit memory (or the ability to effortlessly remember and use information that flows from experience, like knowing not to touch a hot stove) and operates a little like a mental pattern matching game. The brain considers a situation, quickly assesses all your experiences, memories, past learnings, personal needs, and preferences and then makes the wisest decision given the context. In this way, intuition is like an internal traffic light, cautioning you to slow down or stop when a situation isn't good for you or you're not ready and giving you a green go-ahead to move at full speed when something is right.

Along with excelling at picking up on and processing information others miss, Sensitive Strivers have a great capacity to recognize patterns and synthesize different inputs. This means your intuition is more highly developed than most other people because you're constantly adding new data to your bank of knowledge about the world and yourself. Even if you're not actively using your intuition, you still probably experience benefits from it every day. For instance, if you're a manager, getting a read on your direct reports allows you to sense when they're demotivated and to take steps to reengage them. If you're deep into developing a new product, doing a gut check can steer your creative process in the right direction. As a coach, I rely on my gut instincts all the time in my work with clients. Part of my job is to bring order and structure to the thoughts and actions of others, so I tap into my intuition to help me get to the source of what's troubling someone even if they can't find the words themselves.

Intuition can be hard to describe because it's abstract. It tends to be nonverbal and energetic—more like a sense or vibe. But there are some concrete examples of intuition including . . .

- **A gut feeling.** Scientists call the stomach the "second brain" for a reason. There's a vast neural network of 100 million neurons lining your entire digestive tract. That's more neurons than are found in the spinal cord, which points to the gut's incredible processing abilities. Everyone knows what it feels like to have a pit in your stomach as you weigh a decision. That's the gut talking loud and clear. One study found that hedge-fund traders who showed an above average ability to sense their gut signals had greater trading success as a result.

- **Other physical signs.** Your intuition may try to get your attention through other physical signs like lucid dreams or getting sick. Many times in coaching sessions I will notice my client's tone of voice change when their intuition starts coming through. Researchers at HeartMath Institute refer to this as "energetic sensitivity," noting that when it happens, a person's heart rhythms tend to synchronize with the rest of the nervous system, leading to deeper awareness, energy, and composure.

- **Flashes of insight.** Evidence reveals that scientists often happen upon revolutionary ideas *accidentally* by relying on their intuition. This type of innovation-by-hunch is responsible for world-changing discoveries like penicillin and Velcro. When researchers maintain an open, curious mind and allow problems to percolate in their subconscious, they're better able to make creative connections. It's why you get your best ideas in the shower; when your mind is relaxed, your brain's unconscious mode pops on (what psychologists call the "default network"), opening up neural pathways that allow for new connections to form.

- **Synchronicities.** Intuitive thinking stimulates an area of the brain called the reticular activating system, which scans your environment, filtering out unimportant information so that the essential stuff gets through. That's why when you start to consider getting a new job or wanting to land a new client, opportunities suddenly come your way. Your brain is looking for them. Then, when you see the possibilities that were right in front of you, you can take action on your newly available options to create more positive results.

- **A sense of assuredness.** Research shows that pairing intuition with analytical thinking helps you make better, faster, and more accurate decisions and gives you more confidence in your choices than relying on intellect alone. This is especially true when it comes to making major life decisions. In one study, car buyers who used only careful analysis were ultimately happy with their purchases about a quarter of the time. Meanwhile, those who made intuitive purchases were happy 60 percent of the time. That's because relying on rapid cognition, or thin-slicing, allows the brain to make wise decisions without overthinking.

Choosing Intuition Over Fear

It can be tricky to differentiate between intuition and fear. While fear's voice is demanding or restrictive, intuition's is guiding and protective.

For example, fear may tell you to take on a new assignment because you don't want to lose out on a big break. Your intuition, conversely, may be encouraging you to say no because you're already overstretched. In other words, your intuition shows up as nudges that motivate you to act in your best interest. Here's how else to discern the difference.

THE DIFFERENCE BETWEEN FEAR AND INTUITION	
FEAR	INTUITION
Pushing energy, as if avoiding a threat or punishment	Pulling energy, moving toward your best interest
A feeling of frenetic urgency	A calm inner knowing
Driven by insecurity	Driven by confidence and self-trust
Bodily sensation of tenseness, minimizing, or constricting	Bodily sensation of expanding and relaxing
Speaks loudly and dramatically	Speaks quietly, without drama
Thrives in busyness and chaos	Thrives in stillness
Thoughts are reflection of cognitive distortions	Thoughts are reflection of deeper wisdom
Urges you to hide, conform, or compromise yourself	Urges you to shine, move at your own pace, and pursue your needs and preferences

Liz Fosslien, co-author of *No Hard Feelings: The Secret Power of Embracing Emotions at Work*, knows a thing or two about letting your gut lead the way. About four years ago, she was offered the position of executive editor at an early stage music-media company. After the rush of *Someone wants me!* validation wore off, she was faced with a big decision: Accept the position and move from the West Coast to New York in less than two weeks, or let the opportunity pass her by. "I plunged into a confused depression," Liz says, and she anxiously discussed her options with anyone who would listen—friends, mentors, Uber drivers. Like Travis, Liz also bypassed her feelings at first, defaulting to complex, hyper-rational decision-making models. But her exhaustive analysis left her no closer to certainty. Needing to make a decision, Liz finally decided to listen to her gut. When she imagined her life on the West Coast continuing uninterrupted, she felt a twinge of regret. As she imagined life in New York City, grabbing giant pretzels on the streets and getting along with her new coworkers, she felt nervous, but also excited and thrilled. Liz took the job offer, and even though the next two years were tumultuous and filled with drastic changes at the company, Liz never regretted her choice. "Though basing such a life-changing decision on my feeling seemed wildly irrational . . . it wasn't such an idiotic decision after all."

While writing this book, I also had to navigate between fear and intuition. I was invited by a well-known company to be the keynote speaker at an event in New York City. The audience would include many influential people. The catch was that I'd have to write and master a brand-new speech in less than twelve weeks while writing a book and running my coaching practice. As I considered the invitation, I felt torn. Fear of missing out took hold and I wrestled with thoughts, such as, *Figure it out! Make it work! You can't pass up an opportunity like this. You should be happy they asked you.* However, when I processed the decision with a friend, my intuition came through clearly. When I talked about prepping for the keynote and all the sacrifices I would have to make, I felt as if my throat was closing up. When I talked about declining the invitation in order to focus on the book, I felt a sense of relief as if a weight had been lifted off my shoulders. Following my intuition helped me find a compromise that felt spacious and like one I was in full control of. I chose to decline the invitation to keynote, but I decided to still work toward my public speaking goals, which included hiring a presentation coach to help me write a talk and to improve at my own pace. When invitations to speak at major Fortune 500 companies and Stanford University came across my desk a few months later, my intuition gave me the green light, and I felt confident accepting them, knowing I was bringing my best performance to those audiences.

Strategy: Go with Your Gut

When you're faced with a big decision, conventional wisdom says that the right course of action is to gather as much information as possible and to rack your brain for the most rational answer. The problem is that most of the time there is no one *right* answer. There's only the answer that's right for *you*. When you learn to go with your gut, you'll be able to make decisions with intentionality and ease knowing that your choices are a true reflection of who you are.

Intuition is most useful in situations where *analytical* thinking falls short, but going with your gut doesn't mean abandoning logic. Your intuition is actually an advanced form of reasoning because you're integrating data from many sources, both internal and external, rather than just focusing on the kind of objective data that society traditionally values. The next time you have to make a decision, write a simple yes/no question on a piece of paper (handwrite it—this won't work well on a digital device). Focus on a big question that's been weighing on you, like whether or not to go back to school or which candidate to hire for a new position, or if that's too challenging, you can work your way up with lower-stakes questions like where to go to dinner or whether to join an office social event. Make the question as specific as possible. For instance, rather than, *Will more responsibility make me happy?* instead write, *Is it in my best interest to accept the cross-country assignment?* Write *yes/no* below the question, and leave a pen nearby. After a few hours, come back to the paper and immediately circle your answer. Your answer might not be one you like, but there's a good chance that you forced yourself to respond honestly.

Going with your gut is the best way to get clarity on most situations, regardless of how you ultimately decide to act. This is particularly important because Sensitive Strivers tend to burn a lot of energy in the process of making a decision, rather than conserving that energy for implementing the decision they eventually make, which will take at least as much, if not more, focus and thought. Another important benefit from going with your gut is conviction. Studies have shown that people who make decisions based on their intuition have a greater sense of certainty about what they decide to do and feel that their gut-based decisions are a better reflection of their authentic selves. That matters because you likely have many options, all with some unpredictability and all with upsides and downsides. Knowing that you've made the best choice with the information you have helps you mitigate second-guessing and enjoy the path you're on regardless of where it takes you.

If you've always looked to others for guidance, going with your gut will be uncomfortable at first. One of my clients, the owner of a family business, had struggled to make decisions because of his unreasonable concern for how he was seen by others. Out of fear of hurting people's feelings or causing infighting, he had avoided firing underperformers and had neglected to make changes to employee roles and responsibilities. Realizing that his own behavior was contributing to long-standing production issues that had slowed shipping and profits, he decided to act. He was so intrigued by the idea of making decisions from his gut that he planned a "Day of Disinhibition" during which he followed his own intuition about everything he said and did for twenty-four hours.

Going with his gut gave him the courage to start addressing employee conflicts that were contributing to the problem. He found himself making decisions that supported his long-term goals and made time for inconvenient but critical tasks like spending time on the factory floor building stronger relationships with the employees. "It wasn't just what I got done, but how I got it done, how quickly, and how I felt about it," he later told me. "There is something about operating that way that cuts through all the bull. It puts me in the best frame of mind to deal with whatever is in front of me." The experiment was so successful that this founder took his "Day of Disinhibition" to the next level and used it to tackle a wider variety of situations in which he was normally inhibited, such as speaking his mind on issues with his business partner.

Learning to make decisions based on an undeniable sense of integrity isn't an overnight process, but with time, your intuition will get more accurate. The more you practice this skill, the more you'll learn to keep your STRIVE qualities in balance on a day-to-day basis regardless of what's happening around you.

Get Unstuck

1. TEST-DRIVE YOUR DECISIONS. Instead of overthinking a decision, role play it. For two to three days, act as if you've chosen Option A. Observe how you think and feel. Then, for another two to three days, try on Option B. At the end of the experiment, take stock of your reactions.

2. CULTIVATE AN OPEN MIND. Being observant is a Sensitive Striver strength, so use it to keep your eyes and heart open to new ideas, attitudes, and insights. This week, explore a topic just for the fun of it, because it interests you. You can also listen to different music or try a podcast that's way outside your area of expertise.

3. BUILD IN BUFFER TIME. To really hear the insight that comes from inside, you have to build in time to decompress and reflect on your experiences. One way I like to do this is by scheduling at least fifteen to twenty minutes between commitments. This buffer time allows me to simply be with myself and to let my nervous system recorrect after stimulation, so I can integrate and make sense of what's coming through.

4. LIMIT THE DRAIN OF DECISION FATIGUE. You make hundreds of decisions a day—from what to eat for breakfast to how to respond to an email—and each depletes your mental and emotional reserves. The more you can eliminate minor decisions, the more energy you'll have left over for ones that really matter. Creating routines and rituals help conserve your brainpower, as does eliminating certain decisions altogether (i.e., a weekly meal plan, capsule wardrobe).

5. RECALL TIMES YOU TRUSTED YOUR GUT AND IT WORKED OUT. I've never heard a client say to me, "I regret going with my gut." Set aside a few minutes today and list five times you trusted your gut in your life and whether the outcome was favorable. See all those times you were right? Make it easier on yourself going forward by starting to pay more attention to your intuition as a reliable decision-making tool.

Strategy in Action: Travis

In our session, Travis told me that his Sensitivity was as ramped up as it had been in a long time. The many cups of coffee he drank every day, his late nights, and the fact that he hadn't been running as much had left him jittery and irritable. We talked about how to bring his Sensitivity back into balance and, at the same time, how to decide about whether or not to leave his job and dedicate himself full-time to consulting. Travis acknowledged that all his analyses were getting him nowhere and that he was afraid of making a bad decision at this point just because he was so tired of thinking about it.

Together we developed a strategy. On Saturday morning as he was waking up, he opened his notebook and wrote, *Should I go full-time on my consulting business?* And then, instead of starting to work immediately on his freelance projects, Travis went for a long run to give himself quiet time and a chance to access the calm part of himself he knew was there. When he got back, he ate breakfast with his partner and only then did he return to his desk where he had left his notebook. Without thinking too much about it, he circled *no*, and he felt an immediate sense of relief. He thought of the times he had greeted patients in the hospital hallways and they had thanked him for his hard work to keep the medical systems running, and he remembered high-fiving his boss when they rebooted the computer systems after a major electrical outage. He felt a sense of contentment rush over him, both because he could continue to build on those experiences and because he wouldn't have to continue living life on overdrive with a constant sense of pressure and little time for himself.

Now that Travis had some clarity about how to act, he knew he needed to figure out how to move forward, and he used another technique we had discussed in our session (and that you'll try in the Inner Board of Directors Exercise) to help him balance his current emotional and financial needs with his interests and professional goals. His first impulse was to finish his current freelance projects, say no to everything else, and rededicate himself completely to his job at the hospital, but during the next two weeks as he wrapped up his commitments to consulting clients, he tried to keep an open mind about the possible paths forward because he understood more clearly now that there was no *right* answer. The right choice was simply what worked best for him at the moment. With this mindset, he realized that the extra income from consulting was a real plus that had already made it possible for him to make big renovations at home. Plus, he was learning from the consulting, and he didn't want to close the door entirely to the possibility of one day having his own business or using all he was learning at a new position.

After looking at his finances and thinking about keeping his life outside of work more manageable, Travis decided that he could continue consulting if he took on fewer projects, which involved creating the kinds of boundaries we'll discuss in Chapter Seven. He also realized that the unanticipated demand for his time meant that he could raise his prices with confidence and not feel the huge gap in his income that would have resulted from cutting his consulting work in half. The best part of the whole process, though, was that Travis felt a sense of peace that he hadn't felt in some time. He was exercising more, sleeping better, and was able to relax at the end of the day. He had trusted his intuition but also made a deliberate plan that allowed him to move forward in a way that was good for him even if it might not have been the decision someone else would have made.

YOUR INNER BOARD OF DIRECTORS

Imagine a conference table in your mind. Around this table sit the various parts of yourself. Each part represents a board member with certain perspectives, insights, and motivations. Consult your Inner Board of Directors to find answers within whenever you feel conflicted. A direction may immediately unfold, or you may not get a solution right away. But your Inner Board will help you tune into the various aspects of yourself.

INSTRUCTIONS

1. *Identify the problem.* In the center circle, write down a challenge you're trying to resolve or a goal you're currently working toward.

2. *Give each board member a name.* My clients typically have two to four different board members, but you may have more. Common examples of inner board members include:

   - **Your Inner Critic.** Makes you feel worthless and inadequate.
   - **Your Inner Protector.** Cautious, dutiful, on the lookout for unsafe situations.
   - **Your Inner Rebel.** Wants to have fun, and may get resentful toward responsibilities and expectations.
   - **Your Inner Champion.** Grounded, wise, and encouraging.
   - **Your Inner Achiever.** Likes getting things done, but can tend toward overworking and the Honor Roll Hangover.

3. *Understand each board member's goals and attitudes.* Note which voices are stifled, neglected, or quieter than you'd like. You may discover similar feelings and struggles that unite them all. Interview each board member using questions like:

   - What is your job? What function do you serve?
   - How do you think I should approach this problem?
   - What do you hope will happen if I adopt your approach? What do you worry about happening if I don't?
   - Is there more than one way to achieve your objectives?
   - What do you think is my best next step?

YOUR INNER BOARD OF DIRECTORS

Travis

BOARD
MEMBER #1

**INNER
PROTECTOR**

BOARD
MEMBER #2

**INNER
ACHIEVER**

PROBLEM OR
CHALLENGE:

How to balance my
business with my
full-time job going
forward

INTERVIEW: INNER PROTECTOR

What is your job? What function do you serve? My job is to look out for you. I crave certainty, safety, and stability.

How do you think I should approach this problem? Business is risky and not worth it when you have a full-time job.

What do you hope will happen if I adopt your approach? What do you worry about happening if I don't? I hope you'll call it quits with the business so you can focus on growing your career at the hospital.

Is there more than one way to achieve your objectives? You could cap the number of consulting projects you take, like one to three per quarter.

What do you think is my best next step? Decide how much time you can dedicate to consulting, and how many clients you have bandwidth for.

INTERVIEW: INNER ACHIEVER

What is your job? What function do you serve? I'm here to make sure you work hard and push yourself.

How do you think I should approach this problem? The growth you've seen in your business in the last year is exciting. Strike now while the iron is hot.

What do you hope will happen if I adopt your approach? What do you worry about happening if I don't? I hope you'll maximize your consulting opportunities and keep challenging yourself with new and different projects.

Is there more than one way to achieve your objectives? You could raise your prices and be more selective about the projects you take on.

What do you think is my best next step? Adjust prices on your website.

YOUR INNER BOARD OF DIRECTORS

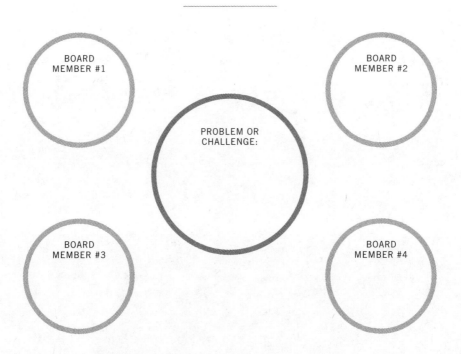

BOARD
MEMBER #1

BOARD
MEMBER #2

PROBLEM OR
CHALLENGE:

BOARD
MEMBER #3

BOARD
MEMBER #4

INTERVIEW EACH BOARD MEMBER

- What is your job? What function do you serve?

- How do you think I should approach this problem?

- What do you hope will happen if I adopt your approach?
  What do you worry about happening if I don't?

- Is there more than one way to achieve your objectives?

- What do you think is my best next step?

BUILD BOUNDARIES LIKE A BOSS

(7)

*"Do not let the behavior of others
destroy your inner peace."*

—DALAI LAMA

JESSICA'S HABIT OF STEPPING IN HAD HELPED BUILD a multibillion-dollar business. She had spent twenty-five years leading, organizing, staying late, and, if necessary, doing the work for everyone else, and now she was in her fifth year as Chief Operating Officer (COO) of a publicly traded retail company. Her identity was deeply intertwined with her status at work, and she moved through the office as if it were her duty to remedy every problem, even if it was below her level or required her to hop on a plane at the last minute. She regularly skipped her kids' school events even after committing to go, and she had even canceled an anniversary celebration with her husband because there had been a crisis at a store opening across the country. Jessica was proud of what she had accomplished, but she also felt a constant sense of resentment that she had come to accept as a necessary consequence of her Inner Drive and Responsibility. At the end of most days, she fell into bed with her husband, who often went to sleep hours before her, after working long into the night at the dining room table. Even though she was constantly exhausted and felt guilty about falling short as a mother, wife, and executive, she kept going anyway, ignoring her growing sense of unease and hoping that somehow the problem would eventually resolve itself.

When we started working together, Jessica told me she wanted to focus on creating a strategy for the company's international expansion. In fact, she had to—Jessica had been given a mandate from the CEO to open five new locations within the next six months even though he knew she was already working fifty-hour weeks and that the longevity of brick-and-mortar retail was uncertain. Jessica complained that she couldn't find space on her calendar for strategy that would contribute to the company's bottom line. When I asked her how she actually allocated her time, she admitted that ever since the company launched its expansion efforts one year ago, she had spent at least half of every day managing the logistics of the store openings, a job that she should have been overseeing rather than doing herself.

When Jessica first started as an associate at the company's flagship location, she had seized every opportunity to go above and beyond, working Black Friday and Christmas Eve each year and attending employer-sponsored leadership trainings. Over the course of ten years, she rose from associate to manager to regional manager to a position at corporate headquarters. Within a few years, Jessica was promoted to VP, but she struggled to let go of former responsibilities because she felt that an important part of her role was to provide cover for her already busy team. Even though the company's relentless growth was a sign of their success, she still felt guilty about the pace of life at the office. Now more than a decade later, Jessica knew she needed to focus on strategy first and foremost. "I have to delegate better to my team," she told me, "but I want to make sure they can do their jobs *and* that everything is done right." Even though Jessica knew her staff wasn't learning to do the work on their own without her oversight, she couldn't let go. Her behavior allowed them to drop the ball and to fail to follow through because they knew Jessica would swoop in to fix the situation.

Like many Sensitive Strivers, the very same STRIVE qualities that had facilitated Jessica's professional rise were now out of balance in a way that threatened to derail all that she had worked for. Each time someone popped in her office to say, *Hey, do you have a minute?* she steeled herself to tackle whatever crisis was coming her way, on top of her already overloaded to-do list. Even when she got some distance by taking a weekend off or a short vacation, she still found herself ruminating about situations back at the office. And now her marriage was suffering, too. Her husband felt neglected and had suggested they consider trying a separation. Even though Jessica loved feeling indispensable, she had come to resent it because it made her frustrated, tired, and now was ruining her marriage. It was clear that Jessica's Responsibility and Inner Drive qualities were dialed up too high. There was only one way for Jessica to help herself, her family, and her team. She had to put a firm boundaries playbook in place.

Say Yes to What Serves You

Boundaries create space between you and another entity, acting like a fence that controls what influences you, what you let in or keep out, and how you choose to respond when someone passes those limits. Unfortunately, creating boundaries doesn't come naturally to Sensitive Strivers because you have a tendency to be influenced by other people's reactions and problems or to put other people's needs and desires ahead of your own. When you do, your own psychological resources get drained. Sensitive Strivers also sometimes make the mistake of viewing boundaries as a bad thing. Fear of abandonment, hurting another person's feelings, or being seen as selfish crop up. Many Sensitive Strivers also feel like setting boundaries clashes with their self-image of being a committed and kindhearted person.

But I'm here to tell you that healthy limits free you up to interact with others in productive ways, to respond effectively to demands on your time and energy, and to focus on doing work you enjoy. Boundaries exist to help you say no to situations, people, and goals that you don't want or don't serve you, so you can say yes to ones that do.

Having healthy boundaries means you:

- **Don't sweat the small stuff.** Take minor annoyances in stride and forgive yourself for slipups.
- **Take responsibility for yourself.** Accept you get to choose your responses and no one—not your boss, significant other, colleagues, or friends—can *make* you do or feel something.

- **Maintain personal standards for excellence.** Don't cave to pressure, comparison, or people-pleasing.

- **Give others the space to succeed.** Avoid *fixing* your team and instead coach them to better themselves even if you sometimes need to ask for or offer help.

- **Be honest about who you are.** Express your preferences around communication, working style, and what you do or don't want out of your career.

- **Follow through on consequences.** If someone crosses a limit, that might mean leaving a meeting, moving your desk, or otherwise reasserting your boundary without embarrassment or apology.

- **Keep promises you make to yourself.** Hold yourself accountable for reaching your own goals, big and small.

RIGID	**HEALTHY**	**POROUS**
Rigid boundaries are inflexible, kind of like a brick wall. Nothing can get in, but nothing can get out either.	Healthy boundaries offer the right degree of protection and flow. They let the good in and keep the bad out.	Porous boundaries are too permeable and don't offer enough protection, as if you had wide gaps in a fence where anything could get in.
Signs: Standoffish, avoids asking for help, feels misunderstood, too protective of information, keeps others at a distance	**Signs:** Self-respect, clear about what you hold yourself responsible for, selective about situations and people you get involved with	**Signs:** Says yes too much, overshares information, overly involved in other people's problems, feels taken advantage of
At work, can look like: Holding too tight to a project and not inviting feedback	**At work, can look like:** Creating office hours so others don't interrupt you during focused work	**At work, can look like:** Not turning down additional responsibilities outside your job scope when you lack bandwidth
At home, can look like: Refusing to accommodate group plans when it minorly inconveniences you	**At home, can look like:** Instituting a no-technology dinner policy, and sticking to it	**At home, can look like:** Living with noisy, disruptive neighbors without ever speaking up

More importantly, boundaries protect the positive habits you have put in place by learning to find your center (Chapter Four), to name and reframe negative self-talk (Chapter Five), and to trust your intuition (Chapter Six).

Play by Your Own Rules

Boundaries, in other words, are rules or principles that you live by and that help you be your best self, personally and professionally. Without even realizing it, you probably already have some guidelines in place that govern how you live and work, but there's a world of difference between subconsciously following rules and deliberately constructing and experimenting with boundaries. While writing her book *The Happiness Project*, author Gretchen Rubin found that one of the most challenging—and most helpful and fun—tasks that she did as part of her mission to create more joy was to identify the overarching principles she lived by. The first of those was the ultimate boundary: "Be Gretchen." It was first because Rubin always found it hard to be who she was. "I have an idea of who I *wish* I were," she wrote, "and that obscures my understanding of who I actually am." Sometimes she would pretend to enjoy activities and subjects that she really didn't enjoy—wine, shopping, cooking—and to ignore her true interests and preferences. To Rubin, "Be Gretchen" meant accepting her true likes, dislikes, temperament, and preferences not only for operating in her personal life but also for operating in her career. After all, her inspiration to "Be Gretchen" originated from a conversation with Justice Sandra Day O'Connor about the secret of happiness in which the Supreme Court Justice pointed to "work worth doing." For Rubin, that meant moving away from a *safer* career in law toward a *riskier* life as an author. As she made the transition and practiced living by her own rules, it got easier to do things like:

- Send a friendly email to a book critic who gave her a negative review (to which the reviewer replied, applauding her for taking it in stride and mentioning he struggled to do the same)

- Take pleasure in—instead of discouraging—her impulse to take pages of notes while researching even if it slowed her down
- Start her blog by focusing on writing one post a day, six days a week, rather than spreading herself thin across multiple business projects

One of my clients was so inspired by Rubin's declaration to "Be Gretchen" that for a milestone birthday she got "Be [her name]" tattooed on her arm where it would serve as a reminder to be true to herself. Since then, that client has felt emboldened to ask for (and get!) special assignments that interest her and to even create her own job description that was a better fit for her strengths (for which she was awarded a six-figure salary). Being herself also translated into greater authenticity, which created more trust between her and her team and allowed her team to be themselves as well. This client no longer felt like she had to spend valuable energy hiding the quirky parts of her personality. She could redirect her efforts into fully owning her leadership and personal style, first by leveraging playfulness and humor in the way she coached her team and then by dyeing her hair a vibrant color and redefining what it meant to look *professional* enough.

Strategy: Follow the Four Feelings Test

My clients often ask me where to start when they're trying to set boundaries and I tell them, as with most things, it starts from the inside—by using the data found in your emotional responses. Remember in Chapter Four when we talked about how, once you're in a calm state, you can heed the messages your emotions are trying to send you? Well, this is where that work gets applied. There is a simple internal assessment I created that has served my clients well: If you have one of four feelings—tension, resentment, frustration, or discomfort—it's a sign that a boundary is needed. By addressing situations where the Four Feelings arise, you create time and space for more of what you do want and less of what you don't.

TENSION

Presents as: A sense of pressure or strain that leads to persistent nervousness, dread, or distraction.

Signals: You perceive that something at stake is dependent on the outcome of your performance. You feel responsible for a situation.

Pros: The ability to perform under pressure is a desirable leadership skill for a reason, because it activates your attention or focus on a task.

Cons: Unresolved tension can mean that you never allow yourself to be still, rest, or recharge because you feel that you must always be moving to meet the next benchmark (either set by others or self-imposed).

Questions to consider: What situations trigger a feeling of dread? What wisdom is my body trying to show me about where I'm overloading myself?

RESENTMENT

Presents as: Long-term, persistent bitterness, indignation, or jealousy you feel every time you think about a situation or interaction. Feeling unappreciated or under recognized.

Signals: Resentment is unvoiced anger. It's a signal that an important rule, standard, or expectation in your life has been violated by somebody else (or maybe even neglected by you).

Pros: Resentment is a choice, which means you can let go of old hurts and take steps to stand up for yourself and rectify imbalances.

Cons: Resentment makes it virtually impossible to exercise empathy or approach situations objectively. It can increase self-pity, not problem-solving.

Questions to consider: Where do I think I'm being treated unfairly? How can I clarify and express my expectations in a courageous way? What, if anything, do I need to work on letting go of?

FRUSTRATION

Presents as: Being upset, annoyed, or displeased at someone else or yourself as a result of being unable to change or achieve something. Feeling blocked or held back in your pursuits.

Signals: Your current approach is no longer working, so it's time to pivot. Or you're doing the same thing over again and expecting a different result.

Pros: It tells you you're going after something that's significant to you but that your brain believes you can be doing something better to achieve your goal.

Cons: Frustration can lead you to give up and resign yourself to less than what you really want.

Questions to consider: What can I control? How can I be more flexible in my approach? What small thought or behavior can I change today that will start to make a difference?

DISCOMFORT

Presents as: A lingering or low-grade sense of uneasiness, impatience, guilt, or even embarrassment. Usually accompanied by your intuition telling you that something isn't *right*.

Signals: When you feel uncomfortable, this is a signal telling you that you need to clarify what you want, then take action in that direction.

Pros: Mild, intermittent discomfort can be a sign that you're pushing and challenging yourself to try new things and experiment, or can serve as a catalyst to change circumstances you're unhappy with.

Cons: Excess discomfort does not lead to growth. Pushing yourself beyond your limits is a surefire path to exhaustion.

Questions to consider: Where am I forcing myself to do something that I'm not okay with? What situations zap my energy or leave me feeling unsettled?

Does every situation where the Four Feelings arise deserve a boundary? No. But look for patterns and recurring themes. That will point you toward opportunities to create new rules and make changes so you can protect your inner life. And since approaching boundaries through the lens of emotions is new, here are a few common examples of how the Four Feelings show up. These scenarios are meant to be a starting point to get you thinking about the domains where Sensitive Strivers struggle setting limits the most: work, personal life, health, and their relationships with themselves. Check off the scenarios that apply to you. The Exercise that follows will help you translate your insight into action and help you generate other examples of where the Four Feelings are coming up for you.

WORK

- ○ You want recognition for your contributions.
- ○ You're working longer hours than you're comfortable with.
- ○ You feel like you must respond immediately to emails.
- ○ You're upset a colleague went behind your back or above your head.
- ○ You're being put in the middle of workplace politics or gossip.
- ○ You're being overlooked for new projects despite stellar performance.
- ○ You're being asked to do more tasks than you can reasonably handle.

PERSONAL LIFE

- ○ Your family isn't respecting time you've told them you need for work.
- ○ You're shouldering more than your fair share of household chores and responsibilities.
- ○ You're responding to emails or taking calls on weekends during personal time.
- ○ Your partner publicly shares details of your personal life that you're not comfortable with or reveals private company information.
- ○ You're being pressured by relatives to hit certain life milestones (have a baby, buy a house, etc.).
- ○ Your friends rely on you to solve their problems or do favors at a moment's notice without the same empathy or help in return.
- ○ You're surrounded by people who criticize or mock things that make you happy.

HEALTH

- ○ You keep food in the house that goes against your dietary goals.
- ○ You want to exercise a certain amount each week.
- ○ You're not letting yourself rest when you're tired.
- ○ You want to limit your caffeine and alcohol intake.
- ○ You stay up later than you want and feel tired in the morning.
- ○ You'd like to make decisions about how you'll eat when you go out.
- ○ You don't want your body or weight to be a topic of conversation.
- ○ You want to make time for restorative self-care practices like meditation.

RELATIONSHIP WITH YOURSELF

- ○ You check social media every time you're bored.
- ○ You don't feel good about the content (TV, news, etc.) you consume.
- ○ You want to stick to your budget and only buy what's on your shopping list.
- ○ You routinely sacrifice hobbies and passion projects.
- ○ You'd like more alone time.
- ○ You don't want to have to pretend to be cheerful all the time even if you feel down.
- ○ You want to get better at not taking things personally.

Get Unstuck

1. PACE YOURSELF. Aim for boundaries that feel doable and easily action-able. Like everything in this book, the goal is steady, incremental progress. That way, you can abide by and follow through on your personal rules, earning credibility with yourself as someone who honors your own needs and desires.

2. IDENTIFY WHO NEEDS TO KNOW ABOUT YOUR NEW BOUNDARY. Typically, this includes the people closest to you and those you interact with on a regular basis—your team, manager, clients, family, or close friends. For example, you may need to inform your spouse that you need quiet time to decompress after work before talking about each other's days.

3. ANTICIPATE PUSHBACK. When you disrupt the status quo, others may not like it. They may try to shame you or convince you to change or lighten up. Don't let them sway you. Stay grounded in what you know is best for you and consistently assert yourself (more on that in Chapter Twelve).

4. SHIELD YOURSELF. Think of your boundaries like a bubble that shields you from others' negative reactions. Claire Wasserman, founder of Ladies Get Paid (and author of the book of the same name), once shared with me that she envisions painting her body in gold armor before entering a tough negotiation or stressful conversation where she'll need to create boundaries. Another great visualization is zipping yourself up energetically. Place your hand by the bottom of your stomach, then draw an imaginary line up your body to the top of your head, as if you were zipping up a coat.

5. GET READY FOR GUILT. At first you may feel apologetic for express-ing your needs. Don't (and we'll get to what to say instead of sorry in a moment). Practice the reframing tools you used in Chapter Five and remind yourself, *It's okay to set boundaries* or *Just because I feel guilty doesn't mean I've done something wrong.*

Strategy in Action: Jessica

In our next coaching session, we sat down and I took Jessica through the Four Feelings Test. Her resentment was closest to the surface, which stemmed from feeling taken advantage of and disrespected. Jessica noticed herself often saying things like "The CEO walks all over me," or "My team makes me feel like a pushover." In reality, no one was *making* Jessica feel anything. Other people may have influenced how she felt, but she was the only one in charge of her emotions. Instead of wasting energy complaining about the behavior of the CEO and her team, she decided to accept and act on her resentment in a healthy and productive way. Specifically, she identified that skipping family commitments was no longer acceptable to her. Jessica blocked off her calendars and listed herself as unavailable starting at 4 p.m. on Mondays and Wednesdays so that she could end work on time, pick up her kids, or head to their games and other after-school activities. She was also committed to spending more time with her husband, and she earmarked Thursdays for date night.

At first, the CEO and her team found these new boundaries difficult to accept, and Jessica was on the receiving end of several huffy emails asking why she hadn't responded to questions and concerns immediately. Her instinct was to jump back in, especially because she felt guilty for being less available, but instead she reminded herself that she was making space for her family and for the high-level responsibilities that were critical to succeeding at the next phase of her job. After a few weeks, her employees and colleagues settled in to her new schedule, and her team stepped up and got the work done without her. She was forced to acknowledge that stepping back was good for everyone, not only because her colleagues were capable of doing the job, but also because she was undoing a culture of overwork that she herself had unwittingly created. Now, her boundary setting had influenced others, and her team was clearly more productive, but also happier than before, knowing that they needed to not be always *on*.

Identifying and enforcing her boundaries wasn't a one-and-done deal with Jessica, but to avoid overwhelm, we focused on implementing one boundary at a time, starting with those where her levels of tension, resentment, frustration, and discomfort were most intense. As Jessica kept the promises she had made to herself about being more present for her family, she realized that without regular, adequate sleep she would never be at her best, so she committed to starting to get ready for bed at 10 p.m. and turning the lights off by 11 p.m. during the week. Although she was initially worried about the lost work time, being well rested actually made her *more* efficient, and she was able to incorporate more time into her schedule to work on the strategic direction of the company. Jessica felt an enormous sense of agency because she had built up a playbook of strong boundaries that strengthened and supported one another, so she continued to make changes when needed. For example, after she made the changes to her schedule, she also implemented something I call "Try Three and Then Ask Me" whereby she taught her team to consult three other people—a coworker, a subject matter expert, the internet—before asking her. While the action was external, it represented an internal shift in the way Jessica valued her time and energy.

You might not have Jessica's seniority and the ability to dictate your schedule—that's okay. No matter the stage of your career, you can still influence situations without authority. For example, talk to your boss about prioritizing the projects on your plate. Privately rehearse responses like, *I have a big deadline approaching, and I'm completely focused on that. Please ask Angela for help*, or *I can work on that after I complete this report*, so you have go-to responses when others ask you to take on more. Be proactive about establishing time frames that work for you, instead of waiting for other people to lead (*I am free to help on Tuesday from 10 a.m. until 12 p.m.*). Practicing phrases like these and the ones in the callout box that follows will make setting boundaries feel much more natural and can alleviate the fear of damaging your relationships. And don't ever forget that your mindset, your attitude, your feelings, your habits, and your decisions are always within your control.

Speak Up Shortcuts

Boundaries are useless unless people know about them. Use the following prompts as starters to deliver your boundary in a strong but diplomatic (and unapologetic) manner.

- I don't want to _____.

- I've decided to _____ instead.

- To ensure I'm [at my best, able to serve you], I'm _____.

- I'm not able to _____, but what I can do is _____.

- Because _____ is important to me, I'm honoring that by _____.

- Right now, I'm saying no to _____, so that I can say yes to _____.

- What I need is _____.

- I'd like to make a request that _____.

- I appreciate you thinking of me. I have to decline _____ to focus on my other commitment of _____.

- I would love to be able to _____, but it's not possible right now. Can I make a suggestion of other people who could help?

- Thank you for thinking of me. I'm not interested in _____.

- I'm flattered and at the same time not able to _____.

- _____ doesn't work for me.

- I have a problem with _____.

- Yes, I do mind _____.

- I'd rather not _____.

- I know we talked about _____, however when I committed I didn't [expect/know about] _____. Because of that, I need to [decline/cancel/postpone] and I appreciate your understanding.

- With the information I now have, I'd like to revisit _____.

BOUNDARIES PLAYBOOK

You may have already noticed a difference in how you show up in the world, so now it's time to use what you've learned about yourself so far to create and communicate the conditions you need to thrive.

INSTRUCTIONS

1. *Think about one major area of your life.* Look back at the checklist in the Strategy or identify another aspect of your life that troubles you. Or you may want to create multiple new boundaries in one area.

2. *Determine where a boundary needs to be set or re-established.* Let the Four Feelings Test guide you. Circle which emotion you're experiencing and complete the fill-in-the-blank. Think about the situation and circumstances under which the emotion arises.

3. *Identify who you are negotiating or setting the boundary with.* Remember, a boundary creates space between you and another entity. Sometimes it's space between you and a coworker or a family member. Other times you may be setting limits between your most balanced self and your self-sabotaging self. In both cases, there may be internal and external shifts involved to follow through.

   - *If you're setting a boundary with someone else.* Externally you'll have to communicate changes. Internally, you may make a decision to spend less time around that person.
   - *If you're setting a boundary with yourself.* Externally you may make changes to the way you manage your calendar. Internally, you may create affirmations or reminders that encourage you to stick to your commitments.

4. *Be clear about how you will support, honor, or uphold the boundary.* Many times in the past you may have tried to set a boundary, but then quickly caved to guilt because it was easier and more familiar. Those days are behind you. Make a clear commitment to yourself about how you'll follow through.

BOUNDARIES PLAYBOOK

Jessica

WORK	HOME
I feel tense / ~~resentful~~ / frustrated / uncomfortable because _work is causing me to miss time with my kids and skip their sports games_.	I feel tense / resentful / ~~frustrated~~ uncomfortable because _my husband asked for a trial separation_.
The boundary that needs to be set is _leaving work by 4 p.m. on Mondays and Wednesdays_.	The boundary that needs to be set is _committing to date night every Thursday to mend our bond_.
I'm going to uphold that boundary by _blocking off my calendar and making myself unavailable for meetings at those times_.	I'm going to uphold that boundary by _hiring a babysitter and picking out activities and events for us in advance_.

HEALTH	SELF
I feel ~~tense~~ / resentful / frustrated / uncomfortable because _I'm constantly under pressure to succeed and unable to rest when I need to. I'm tired all the time_.	I feel tense / resentful / frustrated / ~~uncomfortable~~ because _of the guilt I feel to be a good wife, mother, and leader, all at the same time_.
The boundary that needs to be set is _that I have to build in time to rest. For me that means not working every night until midnight_.	The boundary that needs to be set is _forgiving myself for feeling guilty for the time that I missed with my kids_.
I'm going to uphold that boundary by _starting to get ready for bed at 10 p.m. so that I have time to wind down and then turning the lights off by 11 p.m. on work nights_.	I'm going to uphold that boundary by _reminding myself I'm doing the best I can_.

BOUNDARIES PLAYBOOK

WORK	HOME
I feel tense / resentful / frustrated / uncomfortable because _____.	I feel tense / resentful / frustrated / uncomfortable because _____.
The boundary that needs to be set is _____.	The boundary that needs to be set is _____.
I'm going to uphold that boundary by _____.	I'm going to uphold that boundary by _____.

HEALTH	SELF
I feel tense / resentful / frustrated / uncomfortable because _____.	I feel tense / resentful / frustrated / uncomfortable because _____.
The boundary that needs to be set is _____.	The boundary that needs to be set is _____.
I'm going to uphold that boundary by _____.	I'm going to uphold that boundary by _____.

PART III

ACHIEVE SELF-CONFIDENCE

8

Show Up
as Your
Full Self

9

Aim
Your
Ambition

10

Find
the Right
Fit

SHOW UP AS YOUR FULL SELF

8

*"Going inward. That's the real work. The
solutions are not outside of us. Get to know who
you really are, because as you search for the hero
within, you inevitably become one."*

—EMMA TIEBENS

KATHERINE, THE SENIOR USER EXPERIENCE DESIGNER who you met in Chapter
Four, felt emboldened to think about her own future after the website
launch she led was a success. She had worked hard to stay centered and to
control her Emotionality during the final days before the deadline, and
the client was so happy with the results that they renewed their contract
with her company, saying they enjoyed having Katherine as their point
person and crediting her passion and professionalism as key ingredients
to bringing the project to life. The launch wrapped right before the end
of the year, so Katherine went into her holiday break on a high note. She
took the last week of the year, during which her company was closed, to
do some personal reflection about what she wanted out of the next twelve
months.

When she thought about what she had enjoyed most about her
work in the last year, she realized it all centered on stepping up into
a management role. She felt fulfilled by taking on more responsibility
and having more visibility in the company, but she also realized that

managing more employees would mean actively cultivating her leadership skills, a task she had underestimated until her conflict with Mark. She particularly remembered how fearful and embarrassed she had felt when she had to meet with Beth, and she decided that instead of ignoring those feelings, she could take action to bolster her confidence. During her week off, Katherine dedicated herself to reading books and watching video tutorials about various management techniques, and researching and registering for an online course for new managers. She knew that Beth expected her to deal with Mark, and she thought frequently of something Beth had once said about being a great leader involving more than producing high quality work; it was about bringing everyone on the team along in the same direction. Nothing in her reading or coursework addressed how to do this, and she wondered how she might accomplish it.

With these ambitions in mind, Katherine returned to work. Capitalizing on the natural energy of the new year, her company held an organization-wide strategy meeting to review Q4 earnings and, most importantly, to discuss their goals. This would be a pivotal year, the CEO said in her opening remarks, because in order to achieve their vision of doubling revenue, they would also need to double their workforce from 100 to at least 200 people. The senior leadership team was looking for high performers who were ready to grow their teams, and Katherine felt excited about the way the company's plans for growth dovetailed with her own. Then, the CEO pivoted and spoke about the importance of better defining their organizational culture. As a young company that had grown extremely quickly, they hadn't taken the time to do this, but now they needed to differentiate themselves in the marketplace and operate by certain standards. A list of new company values that included Boldness, Collaboration, and Service appeared on the screen.

Katherine and I had a coaching session about a week after the strategy meeting. Thinking about the company values had made her consider how she fit into the organization as an individual and what she stood for as a Sensitive Striver. "When the CEO started talking about the company values," she said after telling me about her winter break, "I realized that I won't truly be able to lead my team until I can articulate my own values as a person and as a manager." Katherine, always making nuanced connections, realized that seeing her workplace in a new light had created a shift in how she saw herself. "I want to be able to convey what I'm all about with the same conviction our CEO had when she stood in front of the company at the town hall, but that means I have to start owning who I am and what's important to me even if it's uncomfortable at first." Katherine realized that she wanted her team to work toward something bigger . . . together. How to chart her own course, inspire others, and stay true to herself? The missing piece was defining her core values.

Be at Home with Who You Are

While your STRIVE qualities are in your DNA (they are a function of who you are biologically as a Sensitive Striver), your core values are ways of being and believing that help you *take action on* your STRIVE qualities in a manner that brings you into greater equilibrium. Think of core values like your why; they impact every aspect of your life, helping you to show up as your full self, to set and reach personally meaningful goals, and most importantly, to drive the direction your life takes.

For Sensitive Strivers, core values are particularly important because they form the foundation you need to lean into your Vigilance and Emotionality in positive ways, and they help you go from overly concerned with other people's perceptions to channeling your attention inward and pursuing what's right for you. Without clearly defined core values, it's easy to get lost, feel confused, and lose sight of your destination. This is exactly how many clients feel when they initially come to work with me. But, defining your core values restores your own personal navigation system and fortifies your self-confidence. This process is a crucial part of resetting your internal compass so that you can sail toward the kind of success that is going to be most fulfilling to *you*.

Defining your core values may feel abstract at first, but articulating what matters most to you is fundamental to figuring out what you want from your life. Here's why:

- **Core values lessen emotional reactivity.** Let's say you're feeling agitated after a long day at work when nothing went your way. Bringing up a list of your core values can help you in two important ways. First, your core values can help you pinpoint the source of your frustration and understand (not resist or shame) your heightened Emotionality. For example, perhaps you value Honesty and what's causing tension is that you're not sharing your true feelings on an important issue. Using your values, you can check in to figure out what feels off internally and gain perspective on the situation.

- **Core values act like filters to reduce overthinking.** Your values give you a mental shortcut, so you can make intuitive decisions more quickly. Continuing the example above, if you value Health, maybe you lift weights after work to clear your head or perhaps you go home and decompress by cooking dinner with your kids. If you value Positivity, you can look for the lessons from the rocky day. Touching base with your values helps dissolve the internal tension that leads to mental loops.

- **Core values help you show up authentically.** Embracing your core values is a practice of self-acceptance and requires that you be okay with fully being seen. While that's a little scary, it also means you don't have to leave parts of you at home, or masquerade as someone you're not, which is freeing. Fear of failure and rejection begin to lose their power when you bring your whole self to situations.

- **Core values provide fulfilling metrics for success.** Core values, while intangible, give you metrics for success beyond those defined by accolades, achievements, or any other fleeting, external measure. Concern about other people's opinions and disapproval becomes less relevant when you're acting with personal integrity. It's exactly what you need to feel more in control, even when bombarded with society's dominant views on success and happiness.

- **Core values give you stability.** Your core values are the one part of your professional and personal identity you can always count on. In five or ten years you likely won't have the same job title or maybe even be in the same industry, but you do take *yourself* everywhere. Even if you start doing your work in a different way, you are still you. Whenever you question yourself or find yourself at a crossroads, you can always ask what gets you closer to your values.

You achieve inner peace when you feel like the same person at home as you do at work. For that reason, it's ideal for your personal and professional values to be one and the same. Many companies have their own sets of core values, as do many professions such as social work, medicine, and law. The closer you can match your personal core values with those of your company and career, the better, which we'll talk more about in Chapter Ten. But, that's not always possible. Even if your personal values aren't the same as your company's, make sure they're at least *compatible*. If your personal values are diametrically opposed to the company's values, it's a recipe for dissatisfaction.

Know What You Stand For

James Clear, author of the bestselling book *Atomic Habits: An Easy & Proven Way to Build Good Habits & Break Bad Ones,* has spent years studying the art and science of high performance. Several years ago, he created a ritual to document the steps he would take to set a higher standard in his work, lead with honesty, and build a business that serves his audience. James was inspired by the observation that core values are easy to talk about, but much harder to live out on a day-to-day basis. For three years, he created an "Integrity Report," which forced him to revisit his core values and consider if he had been living in a sincere way. "Basically, my Integrity Reports help me answer the question, 'Am I actually living like the type of person I claim to be?'"

In his yearly Integrity Report, James answered three questions:

1. What are the core values that drive my life?

2. How am I living and working with integrity right now?

3. How can I set a higher standard and lead with more integrity in the future?

James doesn't see core values as the end-all-be-all, but rather as another tool in the toolkit to trusting yourself, much like following your intuition. "[I don't] ignore other aspects of my decision-making process. I simply add my core values into the mix. For example, if I'm working on a problem in my business, rather than just asking, 'Will this make money?' I can ask, 'Is this in alignment with my values?' And then, 'Will this make money?' If I say no to either, then I look for another option. The idea behind this method is that if we live and work in alignment with our values, then we're more likely to live a life we are proud of rather than one we regret. . . . If you don't know what you stand for and where you're headed, then it's far too easy to get off course, to waste your time doing something you don't need to be doing . . . that leads you down a dangerous path."

Strategy: Cut to the Core

If you've never given any thought to your core values, don't beat yourself up. It's not something that you learn to do in school. While you may work somewhere that emphasizes upholding company values, it's uncommon for your boss or employer to implore you to look at what drives your own individual identity. Since you can't live your core values unless you can name them, you're going to slow down and do that now. It takes bravery and a healthy amount of self-respect to step away from the frenetic pace of life to define what is important to you. Do this to show yourself just how far you've already come.

You'll need something to write with, a highlighter, and a notebook for this process. Find twenty to thirty minutes when you can focus without distraction. To get into the right headspace, take a moment to ground yourself using your favorite technique from Chapter Four. First, look at the list of values provided. Don't get overwhelmed by the amount of words. Highlight seven to ten that instantly jump out to you. Follow your intuition here and choose the words that resonate with you the most. There is also space to add your own values. As you reflect, close your eyes and think of a time in your life when you were at your best and in complete flow—that is, feeling empowered, productive, and like everything was fantastic. Put yourself back in that moment and feel the energy as if you were reliving the experience. Consider what beliefs lay just beneath the surface of your thoughts and actions in that moment. When you reopen your eyes, circle the core values that you highlighted that were also present during that peak experience. Now narrow it down to three to five core values you must have in your life to experience fulfillment, represent your primary way of being, and feel essential to supporting your inner self. Do a gut check and make sure that every term emotionally resonates with you and gets you in a positive state of mind.

It's a good idea to keep your values somewhere easily accessible so that you can turn to them when you feel lost and unmoored, or simply need a boost. You'll also need them for the Exercise coming up in this chapter. Keep in mind that your values aren't set in stone; they'll evolve as you pass through different life stages and deepen your understanding of yourself as a Sensitive Striver, which is why it's important to revisit them at least a few times per year.

CORE VALUES

Abundance	Compassion	Exploration
Acceptance	Competence	Expressiveness
Achievement	Confidence	Fairness
Adaptability	Connection	Family
Advancement	Consistency	Fearlessness
Adventure	Contentment	Flexibility
Altruism	Contribution	Focus
Ambition	Cooperation	Forgiveness
Appreciation	Courage	Fortitude
Attentiveness	Creativity	Freedom
Autonomy	Curiosity	Friendship
Balance	Decisiveness	Fun
Beauty	Dedication	Generosity
Belonging	Dependability	Grace
Benevolence	Determination	Gratitude
Boldness	Diplomacy	Growth
Bravery	Discipline	Happiness
Calmness	Discovery	Hard Work
Candor	Diversity	Health
Caring	Drive	Helping
Certainty	Efficiency	Honesty
Challenge	Empathy	Hope
Charity	Empowerment	Humility
Cheerfulness	Enjoyment	Humor
Collaboration	Enthusiasm	Imagination
Comfort	Equality	Inclusiveness
Commitment	Excellence	Independence
Community	Experience	Individuality

Inner Harmony	Power	Spirituality
Innovation	Presence	Stability
Inquisitiveness	Proactivity	Strength
Inspiration	Productivity	Structure
Integrity	Professionalism	Success
Intelligence	Prosperity	Sustainability
Intimacy	Punctuality	Teamwork
Joy	Purpose	Thoughtfulness
Kindness	Quality	Tolerance
Knowledge	Rationality	Toughness
Leadership	Recognition	Tranquility
Learning	Relationships	Transparency
Love	Reliability	Trustworthiness
Loyalty	Resilience	Understanding
Mastery	Resourcefulness	Uniqueness
Meaning	Respect	Unity
Mindfulness	Responsibility	Usefulness
Moderation	Responsiveness	Valor
Motivation	Rest	Vigor
Open-Mindedness	Restraint	Vision
Optimism	Risk-Taking	Vitality
Originality	Safety	Warmth
Passion	Self-Care	Wealth
Patience	Self-Control	Well-Being
Peace	Self-Respect	Wisdom
Perseverance	Selflessness	Wonder
Persistence	Service	Other:
Personal Development	Significance	_____
Playfulness	Simplicity	_____
Pleasure	Solitude	_____

Get Unstuck

1. LET IT BE HARD. Every client I've worked with struggles to pick their top values at first. That's okay, and there's a side benefit: When you're willing to stay with the process and allow it to be difficult, you prove to yourself you can do hard things and won't so readily give up on yourself in other scenarios.

2. RELEASE YOURSELF FROM SHAME. Embarrassment has no place in core values selection. You aren't lazy if one of your core values is Self-Care or Rest nor are you unreliable if you value Flexibility. I had a client struggle with feeling vain and narcissistic because Beauty was one of her core values. Counterintuitively, once she stopped resisting it and took steps to incorporate more beauty into her life (redesigning her workspace and taking daily walks in nature), her mood and attitude transformed.

3. BEWARE OF ASPIRATIONAL VALUES. You do yourself a disservice if you select your core values based on how you *think* others perceive you or if you pick the values of a person you wish to be more like. If a value is inconsistent with your identity and not personal to you, it will simply cause tension.

4. LOOK FOR THEMES. If you're having trouble narrowing down your values, try grouping similar terms together. You can ask yourself questions like, *Does this value define me at my best? Do I use this value to make hard decisions? Would I fight to defend this value?* It might seem morbid, but it's also very potent to ask yourself if these values are the ones you'd want read at your funeral.

5. TWEAK THEM. This process is not set in stone, so don't let perfectionism get the better of you. Do one pass, set your results aside, and sleep on it. You can always come back and tweak your values as you gain more insight into yourself as a Sensitive Striver.

Strategy in Action: Katherine

During our coaching session, Katherine eventually culled her list of core values down to her top three, which were Commitment, Curiosity, and Growth. I prompted her to think about how she could use her values to bring her STRIVE qualities into greater balance (which you'll work on in the Exercise). Namely, how could her values help her balance her Emotionality? Knowing that she valued Commitment, it became clear why Katherine had been so bothered by the situation with Mark. Mark's behavior violated her values and undermined her work and her relationships with her colleagues. Clarifying the importance of Commitment helped Katherine create a new boundary—that she'd speak up if Mark went over her head again.

There was no way to anticipate exactly what he would do next, but she felt more confident knowing her emotions weren't misplaced; they were an extension of what was deeply important to her. Even though she didn't *do* anything, defining the boundary helped her move closer to Curiosity. Knowing she had a game plan, she could not only return to the playful part of design that she loved, but also could approach the situation with Mark differently and experiment with new ways to communicate and to build their working relationship. Katherine also decided to honor her Curiosity by keeping a simple mood tracker using an app, so that she could learn more about her Emotionality and herself as a Sensitive Striver.

About a week after the strategy meeting and our coaching session, Katherine participated in a company culture workshop for managers facilitated by Beth. At the front of the room were the company's values—Boldness, Collaboration, and Service—listed on a whiteboard. Each person received two sets of sticky notes: On green sticky notes, they were to list behaviors and actions that supported the company values, and on red sticky notes they were to write down examples of value derailers, or actions that didn't help the company move closer to a culture based on Boldness, Collaboration, and Service. After ten minutes, the whiteboard was plastered with green sticky notes listing positive behaviors, but not a single person had used their red sticky notes.

Katherine knew that the situation with Mark was an example of a derailer. She sat with discomfort for a moment, noticing that she was worrying about what her colleagues might think of her and her capabilities as a manager. In that moment, Katherine asked herself how she could act in a way that would fulfill her personal values. The answer was clear: She needed to place the first red sticky note on the whiteboard. While she had attempted to hide the situation with Mark from Beth earlier, she had learned from her management and leadership work that real leaders grow by being authentic and transparent. She walked up to the board and placed a red sticky that read "team miscommunication." The room went quiet, and Katherine described the situation with Mark to the other managers, who listened and offered suggestions for how to have a candid feedback conversation with him. In the past, she wouldn't have said anything or would have overthought contributing at all. Instead, now she felt assured because she was following her own sense of what was right, not being held back by her fear of what others might think of her.

Beth approached her after the workshop and said how she had perfectly modeled Boldness (by speaking up) and Collaboration (by having a plan to work with Mark and grow her team). She asked if Katherine wanted to co-lead a workplace culture committee where she would be instrumental in guiding the company's mission and vision as it continued to grow. Katherine gladly accepted. She was pleased to put her sense of Vigilance and Responsibility to work in service of not only the company's goals but also the personal growth that would come from making a contribution that was meaningful.

THE WHEEL OF BALANCE, NOW WITH CORE VALUES

It's not enough to simply define your core values. Implementing your core values into how you show up day-to-day involves revisiting the Wheel of Balance you created in Chapter One and continuing to balance your STRIVE qualities by using your core values as guides.

INSTRUCTIONS

1. *Create a description for the core values you chose.* Explain what that core value means to you. Think ten words or fewer. Put this aside; we'll come back to it in a moment.

2. *Revisit the Wheel of Balance.* How did you rate yourself on each of the STRIVE qualities? Reflect on how you've grown in each area, specifically the changes you are most proud of.

3. *Complete the Wheel of Balance again.* It's okay if your score has only gone up a point or two, or even if your measurements are the same as before. Draw one line for where you are now and another line for where you want to be six months from now, just as you did in Chapter One. Write down your growth gap.

4. *Look at your core values and Wheel of Balance side-by-side.* Think about how to increase your scores and move toward greater balance by using your core values. List the actions you can take.

5. *Repeat this process for each of the STRIVE qualities.* By the end you'll have a set of tangible actions you can take. Circle one to start with that you can implement this week.

6. *Reassess regularly.* You'll revisit your Wheel of Balance again before the end of this book, but consider making this check-in a regular process. I suggest doing it at least once a quarter; however, I have clients who incorporate it into a weekly or monthly review. Create a reminder now so you don't forget.

THE WHEEL OF BALANCE, NOW WITH CORE VALUES
Katherine

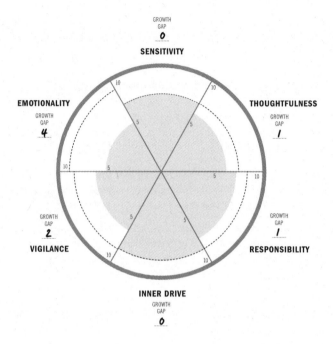

CORE VALUES

1. **Commitment:** Demonstrating I care about my work and my team
2. **Curiosity:** Being open-minded and better understanding myself and others
3. **Growth:** Advancing as a manager

ALIGNING ACTIONS

- Set a boundary with Mark
- Start using a mood tracking app
- Continue leadership classes
- Speak up even if it exposes that I'm still learning

THE WHEEL OF BALANCE, NOW WITH CORE VALUES

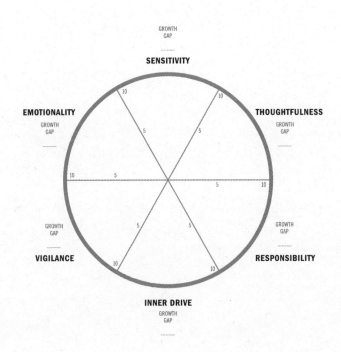

CORE VALUES

1. _____

2. _____

3. _____

4. _____

ALIGNING ACTIONS

• _____

• _____

• _____

• _____

AIM YOUR AMBITION

9

*"And now that you don't have to
be perfect, you can be good."*

—JOHN STEINBECK

IN CHAPTER TWO, YOU LEARNED ABOUT THE HONOR ROLL HANGOVER and gave up goals that were no longer serving you. Since then, you've reclaimed what success means to you by managing your thoughts and emotions, trusting your gut, and building boundaries. Now it's time to rethink ambition and the role it plays in your life, so you can honor your Inner Drive without abandoning your inner peace. After all, if you let your ambition run amok, it'll run away with you. But if you use it to craft goals in a structured way that accommodates your needs and tendencies, you can achieve greatness on your own terms.

Once you've done the work from Chapter Eight, then you're in a position to choose goals that feel fun and exciting, and fit with what matters to you. You now have the opportunity to establish a new goal-setting framework—one that still allows you to achieve, but without going against who you are as a person or sending you back into the many destructive habits you have worked to undo.

Setting new targets to reach the next stage of her career is where Kelly, the Vice President of Programs, Operations, and Administration you met in Chapter One, found herself a year following her return to work after taking a medical leave. She and her colleague had brought on additional staff to tame their workload and had instituted more efficient processes that kept Kelly and others on the team from being overwhelmed and overworked. Through our work together, Kelly had learned to balance her STRIVE qualities to honor her own strengths and sensitivities, and had also come to understand the importance of using her core values to guide her actions. Defining her core values, which included Vitality, Balance, Generosity, Structure, and Contribution, helped Kelly focus her time and energy on what mattered most to her and to break free from the people-pleasing that had led her to burn out in the first place. She had reached a place of relative stability, and after more than a year of working together, we were now meeting once a month instead of every other week. Our conversations had turned to the next step of her professional journey especially because she had been recognized as one of the top managers at her agency and was getting messages from recruiters. And now, she actually had the enthusiasm to consider her future!

Knowing that the Executive Director of her agency would be retiring in the next three to five years, Kelly decided she wanted to position herself as his successor. She knew that getting on the board of another organization would elevate her professional reputation, public profile, and sphere of influence. The boost in credibility could launch Kelly into the top seat at her agency and give her the experience she would need to one day start her own nonprofit providing vocational training to teens who couldn't afford college—a long-term dream she had for her encore career in retirement. Each of these goals—becoming the agency's Executive Director, becoming a board member, and starting her own nonprofit—all lit Kelly up and synced with her value of Contribution because they would allow her to use her skills and give back in a high-impact way. To start getting board opportunities, though, Kelly needed to build her network, notably by attending more local women's leadership events in her area.

Kelly decided to start right away after one of our sessions, and her first instinct was that she should go to one event per week. One event didn't sound like too much, she thought; however, by the time we talked at the end of the month, she had realized that her plan wasn't going to work. On top of her eight-hour days at the office and her workload, which included overseeing the programs for a county with more than eight million people, Kelly had also been on a weight loss journey (a step she took to honor her core value of Vitality), attending fitness classes and a weight-loss support program that helped her lose ten pounds in twelve weeks. On Mondays and Thursdays, she had spin class. On Tuesday, she had her support group meeting, and on Fridays, she had dinner and a movie night with her husband and daughter. So that left Wednesday as her only free evening. Most of these networking events were between 6 and 9 p.m., meaning that if the events didn't fall on Wednesday, she would have to skip one of the other activities on her schedule. On top of that, going to events meant that she got to bed much later than usual, woke up groggy, and struggled with her nutrition goals in the face of rich dinners and alcohol. After a month, her weight loss had plateaued, and her husband was concerned that she was falling back into the kind of patterns that had led to the stress and health problems that had forced her to take medical leave. Not only was Kelly not getting to an event every week, but she was slipping on her other goals and disappointed with herself. In our next session, the first thing Kelly said was that she had made a mistake and that she understood more clearly than ever how important it was to craft her life around her core values of Vitality and Balance. She didn't want to fall into her old habits again. She wanted to set herself up to succeed, not to fail.

Quit Moving the Goalpost

When it comes to setting goals, many Sensitive Strivers fall into the habit of "moving the goalpost." To understand this, imagine a football field. Moving the goalpost is like trying to kick a field goal from the 20-yard line, only to move back to the 30- or 40-yard line when you miss it. You make it more difficult for yourself and tire yourself out in the process. You might notice that you do the same with your goals: Before you've even accomplished one goal, you have already raised the stakes on what qualifies as success. Not only are you virtually guaranteed not to hit the target, but you're also left with an even greater load on your sensitive nervous system. The bigger the goal, the more opportunities to get overwhelmed.

Aiming your ambition, then, is all about setting smaller goals, and working toward them systematically, so you can preserve your energy and go further, more sustainably. In truth, pursuing any goal is filled with starts, stops, and setbacks, and you need a method that fosters your confidence to cross those chasms. The solution is to tier your goals by creating degrees of achievement. Let me be clear: I'm not telling you to play small or settle for less. Rather, you want to chunk your goal down to varying levels, so that reaching it isn't all-or-nothing.

There's a number of benefits to this approach:

- **It allows you to achieve regular wins.** Your goals are likely complex and multilayered, which means they'll take time to accomplish. Getting positive feedback along the way stokes your motivation and keeps your morale high, even when the going gets tough.

- **It helps you focus on execution, not overthinking.** Instead of starting with a big goal that's overwhelming, you ramp up to it. This helps you stay motivated and believe in yourself as you hit smaller checkpoints along the way.

- **It forces you to define what *good enough* and *too much* look like.** By designing a base goal, you give yourself a minimum level of achievement to aim for. Setting a goal ceiling, on the other hand, means you get away from the mindset that *more is always better*. You can make a conscious choice to work within the upper limits of your energy levels, honoring your Sensitivity.

- **It channels your Inner Drive so you hold your goals lightly.** Over-attachment to your goals leads to suffering. But tiering your goals helps gamify your ambition, so you can approach it with more fun, ease, and lightness. You compete with yourself instead of other people.

The best part about tiered goals is that they're effective. Work by BJ Fogg, Director of the Behavior Design Lab at Stanford University, proves baby steps can kick-start your progress and build up to bigger pursuits. Fogg advocates for "tiny habits" or picking "a small step toward your goal—a step so tiny, you'll think it's ridiculous." Your goal is to floss? Start with one tooth. Need a new job? Send one LinkedIn request. Want to start meditating? Take one deep breath. Being classic overachievers, most of my clients balk at this approach, but soon they find that the research doesn't lie: A whopping 91 percent of people say tiny habits increase or greatly increase their confidence. Better yet, there's a snowball effect—65 percent of people say that tiny habits ripple out to create other positive changes in their lives within just one week. That's because the momentum you gain from mastering tiny habits gives you motivation and energy to crush bigger goals. Tiny habits work because they leverage what psychologists refer to as "goal gradient," or the idea that your confidence is either lifted or dragged down depending on your ability to make progress. In other words, the perception of moving ahead propels you toward your goals faster.

BECOME YOUR BIGGEST FAN

Achieving your goals is great, but you'll never gain confidence from them if you simply move on to the next thing and don't pause to celebrate your wins. Psychologically speaking, celebrating your accomplishments isn't frivolous; when you do so your body releases endorphins that reinforce a feeling of competence. Don't wait for someone to acknowledge you, and quit restricting celebrations to epic wins only.

1. CREATE A BRAG FILE. Keep a log of your wins at work (Word or Google document, Evernote note, email folder), so you can look back with a healthy sense of pride. Your brag file can help you better understand your skills and what type of work you most enjoy doing, and even comes in handy for performance reviews or job searching. One of my clients kept her brag file in a fancy notebook and would give herself gold star stickers for her accomplishments.

2. REFLECT ON YOUR HIGH/LOW/HERO MOMENTS. It's no secret that gratitude has many benefits, from improved health to better sleep and happier moods, but true gratitude requires you to acknowledge the ups and downs equally. One practice my clients love is called High/Low/Hero: What was the *high point* of your day? What was your *low point* of the day? Who was a *hero* to you today? One of my clients put High/Low/Hero into practice shortly after switching careers to a new industry. She felt out of her element and like an imposter. But going through High/Low/Hero with her partner every night helped her gain perspective that, while there were growing pains, she was making a lot of headway implementing her ninety-day plan.

3. SHARE PUBLICLY. Don't underestimate the social connection and boost of momentum that comes with voicing your successes. You are always welcome to share your wins in our community of Sensitive Strivers, which you can find at melodywilding.com/bonus, along with printable worksheets, templates, and other free resources from this book.

Strategy: The Giant Power of Tiny Goals

Giving yourself some leeway when setting goals may sound counterintuitive, but the key to getting big results is to start small. I coach my clients to devise a tiered approach to pursuing their goals that follows this 3C framework:

On the foundational level, we have **Commit** goals, which are fairly easy to achieve. A Commit goal is one you know you can accomplish. For example, one of my clients wanted to block time for focused work. She led a team of fifteen people, and her day was filled with back-to-back meetings, which gave her no time to get actual work done. At first, she fell into the Sensitive Striver habit of moving the goalpost. She tried protecting two hours each day, which clearly wasn't realistic. When she inevitably failed to set aside the two-hour time block, she felt badly about herself. In our work together, we walked it back, and her new Commit goal became setting aside an hour on Monday and Friday only.

A **Challenge** goal is the second tier. This will stretch you, but not so much that it leads to self-sabotage. For my client, her Challenge goal was blocking off one hour every weekday for focused work. Doing this forced her to make uncomfortable changes, but was still doable given her current bandwidth. It gave her wiggle room to do big-picture thinking, but she didn't feel like a failure if she had a few days where her time blocking went out the window.

Finally, there's your **Crush It** goal. Your Crush It goal comes to fruition if the sun, moon, and stars all align so that your biggest, most audacious aim is met. My client's Crush It goal was to get to a point where she could consistently put aside two hours every day for strategic work. This didn't happen often, but when it did, she felt like a total badass, and got a lot more done to boot.

You can't and won't hit your Crush It goal every day, but you may very well hit your Commit or Challenge goal more consistently. Start by taking the pressure off yourself to accomplish heroic feats and focus on achieving your Commit goal consistently.

Get Unstuck

1. MAKE SURE YOUR GOAL IS WITHIN YOUR CONTROL. Your 3C goals should be grounded in routines or steps you can personally influence on a regular basis. For instance, getting a promotion might break down into a series of conversations you have with your boss. Getting ten new clients could transform into a social media strategy you use to promote your business.

2. TURN IT INTO A QUESTION. If you're having trouble breaking down your goal into smaller, actionable steps, try adding, *How might I . . .* at the beginning. By reframing your goal as a question, you'll create a list of steps that can be taken to achieve it, which you can plug into the 3C framework. Research shows that framing a goal as questions increases achievement by 27 to 28 percent.

3. DOUBLE THE TIMELINE. Give yourself one year to get a promotion, not six months. Take the quarter to create your website instead of pressuring yourself to do it in a single weekend. Yes, it might take longer, but in all likelihood, the end result is worth the extra time if it keeps you motivated and feeling better about yourself in the process.

4. REMEMBER THAT REACHING YOUR GOALS WON'T BE A STRAIGHT LINE. In Chapter Thirteen, you'll learn more about dealing with setbacks, but for now it's important to realize that you *will* face a period of struggle. So start rallying your Inner Drive's innate perseverance now.

5. DECIDE WHEN TO QUIT. Tim Ferriss, five-time *New York Times* bestselling author, recommends asking yourself, "Can I decide in advance what the checkboxes should be for when I walk [away] . . . ? At what point do the downsides [and] costs end up outweighing the potential benefit of this outcome . . . ? What qualifies as quitting time?" If you don't, he says, "It is very easy to end up persisting and persisting toward a goal that is no longer worth focusing on."

Strategy in Action: Kelly

After I shared the 3C framework with Kelly, she began to see how her initial goal—going to one networking event per week—led her astray. In hindsight, she realized that as she emerged from burnout, the strategy of *going small* had served her well, and she had successfully applied that to strategically prioritize the agency's initiatives and to bring on important hires. It was a natural fit to apply the same method to her own ambition of getting a board seat.

I asked her to pose the question to herself, "How might I accomplish my goal of getting on a board in a way that syncs with my values of Balance, Vitality, Generosity, Structure, and Contribution?" Kelly realized that if she wanted to optimize for Balance and Vitality, she needed to spend her time wisely, only pursuing activities that were the most likely to introduce her to the right type of connections and cutting her commitment in half so that she could focus on going to two events per month, max. She also realized that she could make a more rewarding contribution if she were a speaker at the event. Her final takeaway was that in the course of achieving her own growth, she also wanted to be generous to others in her space by regularly gathering and promoting the ideas of women she admired. Her 3C goals became:

- Commit: Attend one event per month
- Challenge: Attend two events per month and/or speak at an event
- Crush It: Organize and emcee a panel of industry experts

This plan honored her need for structure and allowed her to take productive steps forward, including creating a list of organizations of which she wanted to be on the board, gathering contact information for event organizers, and putting together an email to pitch herself as a speaker. Kelly's persistence soon paid off. Two months later, she sat across from me during our coaching session beaming with excitement. "I almost couldn't wait to tell you, but I've been offered a board seat!" She explained that she had bumped into an old boss at an event who agreed to put her in touch with a new founder looking to round out his board.

"I don't know if I'll accept. There's a lot of due diligence to do," Kelly said, "but the best part is that this all felt so effortless." Kelly realized that by implementing the 3C framework, she could pursue her goals in a smart, strategic way that didn't require her to sacrifice her well-being.

COMMIT, CHALLENGE, CRUSH IT

This Exercise will help you pursue more balanced goals using the 3C framework.

INSTRUCTIONS

1. *Select one professional ambition.* Make sure the goal meshes with your core values and does not show any signs of the Honor Roll Hangover.

2. *Create sub-goals using the 3C framework.* Frame the goal positively, in terms of a behavior or an aim you want to move toward.

   - **Commit.** The minimum of what qualifies as success.
   - **Challenge.** Should feel like a bit of a stretch.
   - **Crush It.** Let your dreams run wild.

3. *Decide what actions you must take to hit your Commit goal.* Master your Commit goal consistently for at least one to three weeks before doubling down on what's working and expanding.

4. *Track your progress.* Experiment to find the method that helps you measure your progress without becoming obsessive about metrics. Below are a few of my favorites:

   - **Weekly or monthly review.** Every Saturday morning, I complete a "CEO Report" that documents quantitative areas in my business (revenue, email subscribers, etc.), plus qualitative data like how I'm feeling, lessons learned, and upcoming projects.

   - **The Seinfeld method.** Comedian Jerry Seinfeld once told a young comedian to get a large calendar and put a big X over each day he wrote jokes. "After a few days you'll have a chain . . . You'll like seeing that chain, especially when you get a few weeks under your belt. Your only job is to not break [it]." Visual cues give you a concrete way to see your progress, motivating you to stay the course. If you prefer digital tracking, I like Stride and Coach.me.

   - **The paper clip strategy.** Another visual goal-tracking tool is starting the day, week, or month with a stack of paper clips, marbles, or coins in one jar and moving them over to another jar whenever you take an action related to your goal.

COMMIT, CHALLENGE, CRUSH IT
Kelly

MY AMBITION IS
To get a seat on the board of a non-profit organization and position myself as next in line as Executive Director of the agency

COMMIT GOAL	CHALLENGE GOAL	CRUSH IT GOAL
Attend one networking event per month	Attend two events per month and/or speaking at an event	Organize and emcee a panel of industry experts

ACTIONS I NEED TO TAKE
Coordinate childcare with my husband for nights I'll be out
Find options for other spin classes to go to
Make a list of events I want to go to
Research contacts to reach out to about speaking and/or being on a panel
Write an email template to pitch myself as a speaker

HOW I'LL TRACK MY PROGRESS
Keep a log in my paper planner of the events I'll go to, who I meet, and who I'll follow up with

COMMIT, CHALLENGE, CRUSH IT

MY AMBITION IS		

COMMIT GOAL	CHALLENGE GOAL	CRUSH IT GOAL

ACTIONS I NEED TO TAKE

HOW I'LL TRACK MY PROGRESS

FIND THE RIGHT FIT

10

*"Designing a career and a life . . . requires the
ability to make good choices and live into those
choices with confidence, which means you accept
them and don't second-guess yourself."*

—BILL BURNETT AND DAVE EVANS

AFTER TAKING AN EIGHT-WEEK HIATUS FROM JOB SEARCHING to detox from her
Honor Roll Hangover and to rebuild lost habits that made her feel good
about herself, Alicia from Chapter Two was feeling more like herself
again. Her malaise had lifted, and she was optimistic about her future,
in spite of the recession. She had space to reconsider her professional
future and the steps it would take to get there even though she was still
nervous about trying to find a new job in the midst of an economic
downturn.

During her break from job searching, Alicia, who had been going
through in vitro fertilization treatments to have a child by herself, found
out she was pregnant, which made her even more motivated to get a
new job and *quickly* so that her professional situation could be settled
before the baby came. As she imagined her future work and career, Alicia
was mindful of the core values she had identified in our work together:
Dependability, Authenticity, and Connection. It was clear that her current role no longer fulfilled her and that if she was going to try to align
her life with the core values she had defined, particularly Authenticity,

she would need to rethink the tasks and responsibilities associated with her position or find a new place to work. Her role at the magazine was also commission-based, which was in opposition to Dependability. The fact that her income varied substantially from quarter to quarter made her uneasy and unbalanced her Emotionality.

Due to the recession, Alicia knew that reimagining her current role would be unlikely. Her boss had recently accepted a voluntary buyout, and now she was reporting to the Senior Vice President of Marketing, who frequently reminded her team that they were all lucky to even have jobs. To make matters worse, her coworkers, who had always been cliquey, were taking it to a new level. They had recently held several impromptu meetings that they *forgot* to tell her about and had made a series of secret decisions that Alicia only learned of after the fact. She had always focused on the sense of Connection she had to her family and especially to her sister, but the loneliness she felt in the office made her realize that Connection was critical to her in every aspect of her life.

As she explored her options, Alicia leaned on her intuition, which told her that the only way forward was a new job in spite of the uncertainty in the economy. The problem was that although she was clear on what she was moving *away* from, Alicia was still hazy on what she was moving *toward*. For much of her career, she had felt like an outsider no matter what the company was like or how well she was getting along with coworkers. Even as she learned more about herself as a Sensitive Striver, when she fell into her old mental habits, her impulse was to invent ways to change herself rather than to consider that it might be okay to find a workplace where she could thrive personally and professionally. The thought of finding a role that better fit her personality felt somewhat indulgent, but picturing herself in a different professional environment filled her with hope, and she felt enthusiastic about crafting a future that allowed her to channel her determination into work that energized her. Unfortunately, she didn't know how to take her STRIVE qualities into account as she sought out a new direction for her career path.

You may know exactly where you're going or you may be like Alicia and a little unsure about how to find contentment in your career, but either way, you're ready to tailor your work to fit who you are, whether you're pleased with your role and simply want to be more deliberate about what comes next and how to get there; whether you feel you could be happier and want help to identify what changes you could make to craft a more satisfying professional life; or whether you feel you want to change everything and start again. No matter where you are in this journey, it's time to be brave enough to consciously find or create the conditions that will allow you to make a bigger impact and experience more satisfaction than you ever thought possible.

Working Conditions That Work for You

Finding a good fit between your personality and your career happens when there's synchronicity between your tasks, the environment you're in, and the value you both provide and receive from your responsibilities. While many people hope to find satisfying work, doing so is more significant for Sensitive Strivers. Recall from Chapter One that your sensitivity means, for better or for worse, that you're more responsive to and shaped by the conditions in which you live and work. According to a study conducted by Elaine Aron and her colleagues, "Sensitive people . . . in a good, positive environment tend to outperform others. They're less depressed, less shy, less anxious, and they're prone toward more positive [emotion] than others." That means that even though you may feel that matching a professional role with your personality is too much to ask for, it's actually essential if you want to keep your STRIVE qualities in balance *and* make an impact.

Other research backs up the theory that personality-job fit is critical. Studies show that when your professional world is consistent with who you are as a person, you experience your work as more meaningful. The effect is greatest when your work matches your values and brings you a sense of self-esteem.

Fitting your career to your personality not only makes you more adaptable and resilient to changing demands, but it also translates to better performance on the job. People with the best fit between their personality and their job earned up to a month's salary more each year because they were happier and more productive. A strong person-job fit is also linked to greater engagement, energy, enthusiasm, and innovation at work.

People who take a proactive approach to find a fit between their role and their needs are also more likely to take initiative in gathering feedback about their performance, negotiate for better assignments, and identify ongoing career opportunities that position them to play to their strengths in the long run.

If you're still unconvinced, consider that it's not just about you. A high-functioning team requires a mix of personalities, so when Sensitive Strivers find roles and workplaces in which they can be themselves, everyone wins. While not every company or manager has figured out how to create this kind of diverse workforce, more than 87 percent of today's businesses are making inclusion a top priority because it results in higher revenue, faster decision-making, and better quality work. The trend toward hiring neurodiverse leaders, or those with certain brain differences, presents a huge opportunity for Sensitive Strivers looking to advance their careers, so remember that your natural aptitudes—compassion, an ability to see the big picture, and loyalty—give you a competitive advantage. Plus, in a work world dominated by automation and increasing incivility, the need for Sensitive Strivers has never been greater. No technology can ever replace your creativity, empathy, and superior sensory perception. When fully leveraged, your smarts, conscientiousness, and kindness are an unbeatable combination that makes you rare and valuable in what psychologist Daniel Pink calls the "high concept, high touch" age. Don't let your gifts go to waste, because the world needs you more than ever before.

STAYING SANE IN A TOXIC WORKPLACE

It's impossible to be effective and at peace in a toxic workplace. Even if you work from home, the negativity of a toxic workplace can transcend physical walls. The drama, dysfunction, and poor communication can eventually affect everything from your personal life and health to your self-esteem. Quitting immediately isn't always an option, so here are a few tips to improve the situation while you devise an exit strategy.

DON'T . . .	DO . . .
LET NEGATIVITY WIN Avoid complaining to your partner or friends. Ruminating about your terrible job keeps you in a pessimistic mindset and prevents you from seeing solutions.	**USE WORK AS A TESTING GROUND** Develop skills and competencies for future opportunities. Utilize free videos or online training if you can't learn what you need to on the job.
PARTICIPATE IN DRAMA Move your desk away from destructive jerks. Get sympathetic colleagues on your side who can tip you off as to what meetings they're in. Limit time with people who gossip.	**FIND SUPPORT** Build a circle of confidants within the office or externally through a professional association or peer community. You need trustworthy people in your corner who can provide a sanity check.
SKIMP ON BOUNDARIES Take your full lunch break. Don't answer emails after hours or work on the weekend. Use your PTO.	**CREATE A POSITIVE WORKSPACE** Surround yourself with images, quotes, and colors that relax you or bring you happiness.
FAIL TO ADVOCATE FOR YOURSELF Think creatively about shifting toxic elements of your job, for example, by delegating, changing supervisors, or switching teams. Find another internal ally who will go to bat for you if your boss isn't supportive.	**PREPARE YOUR EXIT** Focus your energy on your next steps and finding something better. Get your resume in order, reach out to recruiters, and reconnect with your network. Have three to six months of savings in the bank.

DON'T . . .	DO . . .
HESITATE TO DOCUMENT Keep track of inappropriate or abusive behavior so you can report it if need be.	**MANAGE YOUR OWN SELF-TALK** Remind yourself that this situation is temporary and reframe how you perceive it. It's not a crisis; it's a challenge. Your boss isn't intolerable; they're just emotionally immature.
LOSE YOUR SENSE OF SELF Seek a sense of mastery, momentum, and enjoyment from another outlet, such as a side hustle or hobby.	**REMEMBER YOUR JOB DOESN'T DEFINE YOU** Revisit your values and what you stand for outside of your job title.

Strategy: Bring Your Whole Self to Work

Without the right conditions, it's going to be difficult, if not impossible, to live out your core values and to achieve your goals. While some people can bloom wherever they're planted, the best option for Sensitive Strivers is to act with intentionality and agency to find a genuine personality-job fit. In the Exercise at the end of this chapter, you'll get a chance to assess your current role, but before you can decide whether or not it's a true match, you need to define and prioritize what's important to you using The Sensitive Striver's Hierarchy of Professional Needs.

Viewing current and potential roles through the lens of what you need to survive versus what you need to thrive is an opportunity for you and the organizations you work for to go beyond the bare minimum, so that you'll be more effective, satisfied, and impactful at any stage of your career.

THE SENSITIVE STRIVER'S HIERARCHY OF PROFESSIONAL NEEDS

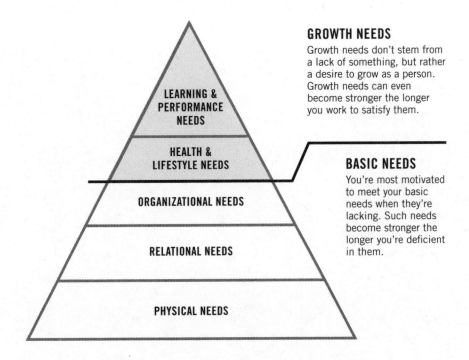

GROWTH NEEDS
Growth needs don't stem from a lack of something, but rather a desire to grow as a person. Growth needs can even become stronger the longer you work to satisfy them.

LEARNING & PERFORMANCE NEEDS

HEALTH & LIFESTYLE NEEDS

BASIC NEEDS
You're most motivated to meet your basic needs when they're lacking. Such needs become stronger the longer you're deficient in them.

ORGANIZATIONAL NEEDS

RELATIONAL NEEDS

PHYSICAL NEEDS

BASIC NEEDS

If you've ever taken a psychology class, you might be familiar with Maslow's hierarchy of needs, which illustrates his theory that individuals can only grow and reach their full potential if certain basic requirements are met. The same idea applies in the workplace to basic versus growth needs. Here's how:

PHYSICAL NEEDS

Physical needs form the foundation of the pyramid and encompass all aspects of your actual workspace whether you work at home or you go into an office. Finding the best level of stimulation balances your Sensitivity and helps you feel stable and at peace while creating an ambience that allows you to focus and reap the best of what your Thoughtfulness has to offer.

Questions to consider

- How quiet or private do you prefer your workspace to be?
- Are you excited or repelled by the idea of working in a high-energy environment?
- What type of atmosphere allows you to feel engaged and present—from the colors and room accents to the lighting?

RELATIONAL NEEDS

This band of the pyramid includes all the interpersonal aspects of your job, from how frequently you interact with colleagues to the sense of trust and belonging you feel in the workplace. While some of the qualities of being a Sensitive Striver overlap with introversion, remember, 30 percent of sensitive people are extroverts, so you may love teamwork or people management even if you also enjoy working alone. Tap into your Emotionality as a way to think about the qualities of your professional relationships that bring you joy and deep satisfaction.

Questions to consider

- How frequently do you want to interact with colleagues?
- How much of your time do you like spending in meetings or collaborating with others, and how excited does that make you?
- What do you need from your workplace relationships to feel like you're accepted and that you belong?

ORGANIZATIONAL NEEDS

The third level of the pyramid (and the last part of understanding your basic needs) requires you to evaluate the type of organizations you would like to work for. Organizational needs include not only the ways in which a company functions like its size, culture, and leadership style but also what it brings to the world, its reputation, and what it stands for in the marketplace.

Questions to consider

- What kind of leader motivates you and is it essential to you that their values mesh with yours?

- How important is it that your company has a mission that you're passionate about?

- What type of organizational culture do you thrive in? One where decisions are made by consensus or hierarchically, for example?

GROWTH NEEDS

Once your basic needs are met, you can begin to think about your growth needs, which stem from a desire to advance as a person.

HEALTH AND LIFESTYLE NEEDS

You don't want to land back in the Honor Roll Hangover, so think about your work-life balance and the conditions that will drive optimal physical and mental health. The key is to take responsibility for the logistics and parameters that govern your energy and your overall well-being.

Questions to consider

- How much control do you need over scheduling your day, and how often do you need breaks?

- What time would you ideally get to work and leave at the end of the day?

- What degree of flexibility can you not live without?

LEARNING AND PERFORMANCE NEEDS

At the top of the pyramid sit duties, skills, and strengths you want to utilize in your work. There is no gold standard because fulfillment in this area looks different for everyone. Some people may meet their needs by pursuing work that is their *passion* while others care about just earning enough to pursue things that matter to them outside of work. Lean into your Inner Drive to reflect on how you aspire to grow in the future.

Questions to consider

- What do you consider to be your special gifts and talents?
- How much do the key tasks associated with your role energize or drain you?
- What interests or skills do you care about getting better at or applying differently?

Knowing what you want and need opens up many possibilities with respect to how you live and work. You don't always have to make radical shifts like quitting your job (that type of huge overhaul can be too overwhelming in one fell swoop for most Sensitive Strivers anyway), but defining both your basic requirements and ideal conditions can help you make small tweaks that create better person-job fit and move you closer to your dreams.

Get Unstuck

1. LOOK TO THE PAST. Consider your past five to seven roles (this can include temporary projects or volunteer gigs as well) and what you liked most about them—what really lit you up? What do you wish you could carry forward or expand on? Recall times when your STRIVE qualities were at a level of eight out of ten on the Wheel of Balance. What was happening? What were you doing? On the flip side, think about what conditions of the job you hope never to deal with again.

2. CHOOSE PRIORITIZATION OVER PARALYSIS. You may find that your needs in certain categories conflict with each other. That's normal. Resist the urge to change everything at once. Pamela Slim, author of *Body of Work: Finding the Thread That Ties Your Story Together*, says, "If certain areas compete, which is a priority right now? Which sacrifices are you willing to make to serve your priorities?"

3. JOB CRAFT. You can also proactively customize your role to find more career satisfaction. If you enjoy educating others, but your job focuses on execution, you could redesign your tasks to include creating training tutorials other teams can utilize. One of my clients crafted her role by setting up a rotation model with her manager, which allowed her to learn new skills and deepen relationships with different stakeholders throughout the company.

4. ZOOM IN. Instead of trying to devise a five-year career plan, try this more manageable thought experiment: Imagine yourself one year from today. What would be different? What would stay the same? You might even have to zoom that time frame down further to six or three months.

Strategy in Action: Alicia

Over the weekend, Alicia headed to her favorite hiking spot so she could reflect on what she ideally needed and wanted from her next role. While the obvious choice for her next step was to continue in advertising, she actively cultivated an open mind as she followed the path through the trees. She saw this moment of transition in her life as an opportunity, but she knew she would have to be more intentional than she had been up until now if she hoped to find a workplace where she could thrive. When she got home that night, Alicia wrote her core values at the top of the page: Dependability, Authenticity, and Connection. Using those values as her foundation, she imagined her next role in light of The Sensitive Striver's Hierarchy of Professional Needs.

Beginning with her basic needs, Alicia considered her ideal physical environment. Much of Alicia's day was spent on the phone, and she preferred working where she could speak freely without worrying about disturbing anyone. Though many of her colleagues raved about working remotely, Alicia preferred a more structured work environment, which for her meant being in an office where she could have some privacy or establishing a quiet, dedicated spot in her home. She noted her observations next to the lowest tier of the pyramid she had printed out for herself.

When it came to relationships, Alicia realized she was deeply unhappy. She didn't need to be best friends with her coworkers, but she wanted to feel a sense of connection and belonging, and she hoped her next workplace would be a psychologically safe space in which all ideas and opinions could be heard. This was especially true because she liked being part of a large team and enjoyed learning from her colleagues.

Finally, Alicia considered her organizational needs. Without a doubt, Alicia was looking for a role that would give her full maternity leave and on-site daycare. She also wanted to work for a manager who inspired her rather than one who constantly threatened her and her team about their jobs. Economic uncertainty would be a given for some time, but she wanted emotional Dependability in the workplace, as well as financial Dependability in the form of a salary rather than a commissions-based paycheck.

When it came to her growth needs, Alicia tried to anticipate what her future as a single parent might look like. Even though she wasn't yet prepared to say exactly what she needed, she had seen enough new parents to know that flexibility was essential in the short run with respect to her hours and the timing of her deliverables. While she knew this might change in the future, when she imagined her ideal role, she wanted a place that understood and accepted that sometimes employees might need to care for a new baby or a sick parent or partner, or might want to take a sabbatical. She wanted to be able to be truthful about what was going on in her life and not have to scramble or hide the fact that she might occasionally need a day off to attend to her child or herself.

Finally, with respect to her learning and performance needs, Alicia closed her eyes and allowed herself to dream. She first thought about past roles, what she had liked, what had worked for her, and what had been difficult. In an earlier role at another advertising firm, she had had the opportunity to work on several campaigns with the marketing and content teams. After that she had moved to sales because it was high status and competitive, but in retrospect, Alicia realized that she might have enjoyed working on more cross-collaborative projects rather than spending the majority of her time courting new accounts. Alicia also drifted back to about a year prior when she had done some event organizing at the pottery studio where she took her classes in exchange for free registration. Even though the barter work wasn't part of her resume and didn't seem connected to her larger professional life at first, it struck her that working with the marketing and content team overlapped with work at the pottery studio because both projects had required her to put together project plans and creative designs and to coordinate with vendors—all of which simultaneously engaged her artistic side and her conscientiousness.

Through this process, Alicia gained enough clarity to revisit her job search with more direction. She had a hypothesis that she might be more fulfilled by a marketing-oriented role at a company that promoted flexibility and had a culture of inclusivity. She recognized that she didn't have all the answers, so she didn't get caught up in perfectionism and try to figure out everything all at once. Instead she left herself open to possibility and let her job search strategy evolve as she gathered more information through interviews and networking. Over the next two weeks, she also reached out to friends to ask for introductions to people who had moved out of sales into other roles, so that she could understand what their experiences had been like. All of this confirmed that marketing would be a good path for her. She dove full force into her career pivot, leveraging her network, alumni group, and friends from the pottery studio. Within a month, Alicia was interviewing for new roles (ones that offered full maternity leave and on-site daycare—two of her nonnegotiables) and was well on her way to finding a position before her third trimester.

What to Do When You Want to Change Everything

Coming to the realization that it's time for a job switch or broader career change? By taking small steps and tending to your emotional well-being throughout this process, you can make a successful transition.

1. DEFINE NONNEGOTIABLES AND NICE-TO-HAVES. Focus on what you *do* know versus what you *don't* know in areas like salary, location, and job duties. Even if it's not a full picture yet, it's still clarifying to know your requirements so you can choose which new opportunities you say yes or no to.

2. TURN WORRY INTO FUEL. List actions you could take to get the information or experiences you need to confirm or disconfirm your concerns. *Would I really enjoy a leadership role?* To find out, talk to a mentor, take a management class, or get a stretch assignment that gives you part-time leadership responsibilities.

3. BE VISIBLE. Update your online presence with your most recent work experiences, achievements, and updated headshot. Craft a new personal brand statement by filling in this blank: *I am* [your role/title] and *I help* [who you work with] *understand/do* [what you help them accomplish], *so that* [the transformation or final result]. Publish content (original or curated) to become seen as a thought leader.

4. DIVERSIFY YOUR STRATEGY. Avoid relying on online job boards alone. Reach out to family, friends, and former colleagues to let them know what you're looking for. Engage recruiters, attend events or conferences, contact your alumni organization, or target employers directly.

5. PACE YOURSELF. Changing careers doesn't happen overnight. It's a messy, iterative undertaking that takes time, patience, and energy. Sensitive Strivers work best with order, so create a reasonable schedule for your job search activities.

YOUR CAREER FIT

Now that you know about The Sensitive Striver's Hierarchy of Needs, you're in a position to evaluate how your current career conditions stack up against your ideal personality-job fit.

INSTRUCTIONS

For each of the following questions, choose how much you agree or disagree with each statement. Your results will point you to the next steps you should consider.

The physical environment where I work reflects my preferences for stimulation.

|————————|————————|————————|————————|————————|
COMPLETELY AGREE   MOSTLY AGREE   SLIGHTLY AGREE   SLIGHTLY DISAGREE   MOSTLY DISAGREE   COMPLETELY DISAGREE

When I'm working, I often get fully immersed in what I'm doing.

|————————|————————|————————|————————|————————|
COMPLETELY AGREE   MOSTLY AGREE   SLIGHTLY AGREE   SLIGHTLY DISAGREE   MOSTLY DISAGREE   COMPLETELY DISAGREE

Throughout my workday, I get to interact with my colleagues to an extent I feel comfortable with.

|————————|————————|————————|————————|————————|
COMPLETELY AGREE   MOSTLY AGREE   SLIGHTLY AGREE   SLIGHTLY DISAGREE   MOSTLY DISAGREE   COMPLETELY DISAGREE

The organization where I work embodies values that I care about.

|————————|————————|————————|————————|————————|
COMPLETELY AGREE   MOSTLY AGREE   SLIGHTLY AGREE   SLIGHTLY DISAGREE   MOSTLY DISAGREE   COMPLETELY DISAGREE

I enjoy the type of impact my work has (i.e., the audience it affects or serves).

|————————|————————|————————|————————|————————|
COMPLETELY AGREE   MOSTLY AGREE   SLIGHTLY AGREE   SLIGHTLY DISAGREE   MOSTLY DISAGREE   COMPLETELY DISAGREE

The culture of my organization is healthy and functional.

|————————|————————|————————|————————|————————|
COMPLETELY AGREE   MOSTLY AGREE   SLIGHTLY AGREE   SLIGHTLY DISAGREE   MOSTLY DISAGREE   COMPLETELY DISAGREE

The activities and tasks that occupy my day leave me feeling energized and fulfilled.

COMPLETELY AGREE   MOSTLY AGREE   SLIGHTLY AGREE   SLIGHTLY DISAGREE   MOSTLY DISAGREE   COMPLETELY DISAGREE

In my career, I get to utilize skills I consider to be strong assets of mine.

COMPLETELY AGREE   MOSTLY AGREE   SLIGHTLY AGREE   SLIGHTLY DISAGREE   MOSTLY DISAGREE   COMPLETELY DISAGREE

My current role offers me opportunities to advance skill sets I want to continue mastering.

COMPLETELY AGREE   MOSTLY AGREE   SLIGHTLY AGREE   SLIGHTLY DISAGREE   MOSTLY DISAGREE   COMPLETELY DISAGREE

Right now, my job strikes the right work-life balance that fits my lifestyle needs and goals.

COMPLETELY AGREE   MOSTLY AGREE   SLIGHTLY AGREE   SLIGHTLY DISAGREE   MOSTLY DISAGREE   COMPLETELY DISAGREE

IF YOU ANSWERED . . .

Mostly disagrees. Start from the bottom of the pyramid by addressing your basic needs first, then work your way up once you have those in a good place. Overall, you're in need of some major changes, so revisit "What to Do When You Want to Change Everything" for more tips.

Some agrees, some disagrees. You have opportunities to optimize your personality-job fit for greater happiness. Start with the areas you rated *mostly disagree* or *completely disagree* and create action steps to address those needs. Check out the point on job crafting in the "Get Unstuck" section of this chapter.

Mostly agrees. Congrats! Your work is a great fit for your personality. The fact that you like your job and are in a great environment means you can concentrate on the tippy-top of the pyramid—your learning and performance goals. Don't lose sight of exciting possibilities, and be open to stretching yourself in the name of deeper meaning and fulfillment.

PART IV

SUSTAIN SELF-GROWTH

11

Take
Smart
Risks

12

Speak Up
and Stand
Your Ground

13

Bounce
Back from
Setbacks

TAKE SMART RISKS

11

*"And the day came when the risk to
remain tight in a bud was more painful
than the risk it took to blossom."*

—ANAÏS NIN

RISK, OR THE DECISION TO TAKE ACTION WITH IMPERFECT INFORMATION, often gets
a bad rap because it's associated with recklessness; however, risk is also
a necessary ingredient for success. Think about it. The Sensitive Striver
who operates on autopilot for thirty years is unlikely to achieve great
things professionally, let alone personal satisfaction. If you want to
reach your full potential, you have to be willing to expose yourself to
unwanted consequences—be it loss, rejection, judgment, or failure. In
fact, a survey of senior executives identified a willingness to take risks
as a key ingredient to their ability to move up through the ranks, especially when presented with an opportunity for which they didn't feel
completely prepared.

Whether you know it or not, you're already well on your way to changing your relationship with risk from one of fear to ease. In each chapter of
this book, you've stepped up to implement new tactics and techniques—
like starting before you're ready, finding your center, embracing your
whole self, and more—each of which has required you to take chances and

bet on yourself. You're now at a point where you can capitalize on your growth and greet challenges ahead with vigor. That's where Jessica found herself about a year after we last saw her in Chapter Seven.

It had been six months since she and her team had fulfilled their mandate to open five new locations, and Jessica could now turn her attention to higher-level strategy, specifically making a recommendation to the CEO about how to steer the company's operations in the next one to three years. Because of the boundaries she had implemented, Jessica was no longer overfunctioning, and most days, she was able to leave work at a reasonable hour to spend time with her family and to mend her marriage. Things weren't perfect yet (and Jessica realized achieving *balance* was in constant flux), but she told me that the confidence she gained through identifying and enforcing her boundaries was invaluable. Each time she said no, stood up for herself, or asked a team member to step up required courage in the face of her nerves. And Jessica found that even if she didn't get the outcome she hoped for, every small risk was an opportunity to feel stronger and more self-assured.

As she reviewed the company sales data, it was impossible for Jessica to ignore the overall downturn in retail, even though their stores were still doing well. She knew the CEO was expecting her to recommend further brick-and-mortar expansion—after all, that had always been the company's main business and her area of expertise—but she couldn't help but see that the future of the company, and perhaps her own future, lay in diversifying its revenue streams. Jessica knew that they needed to catch up with their e-commerce competitors . . . and fast, if they wanted to survive.

You might not be facing global industry trends or contemplating a one-to-three-year plan like Jessica, but I bet that you have faced a crossroads similar to hers that required you to take a risk, however major or minor. Maybe you had a great idea and wanted to share it with your leadership, or thought about volunteering for a project outside of your normal domain. Perhaps on a bigger scale, you've wondered if you should make the leap and take a new job, switch teams, or become an entrepreneur. Taking a risk means making a decision or going after a challenge your intuition says is right because you stand to gain something by doing so, whether that's growth or discovering something new about yourself. Most of the time, the upsides are tremendous in the form of self-worth, income, etc., and the downsides are relatively mild in that they don't pose a threat to your health or safety.

Betting on yourself is not easy, but in this chapter, you'll begin practicing doing it so that you're ready when opportunities do arise and can seize new possibilities without overthinking or sending yourself down an emotional spiral. While you can't completely bypass the fear that sometimes comes with taking risks, you can learn how to work through it, and maybe even have some fun in the process.

You're Stronger Than You Realize

For a long time, you've probably assumed that risk-taking and sensitivity don't mix. While it's true that you may never become a brazen adventurer, you're uniquely equipped with cognitive circuitry that makes you a smart risk-taker. Your STRIVE qualities can help you approach risks in a calm, measured way that leads to better results. Consider this:

- **Use your intuition to aid risk analysis.** Feelings are not in opposition to logical reasoning; they provide essential support for it. The key is using *both* your Thoughtfulness and Emotionality, and not letting one override the other.

- **Only take risks when it matters.** Follow your sense of Inner Drive and Responsibility to pursue risks that are personally meaningful to you. Studies show that people accept risks because they value an activity and view it as important because it makes a contribution.

- **Value your perceptiveness as a tool.** Your Sensitivity and Vigilance mean you process and synthesize more input than the average person. Let go of any lingering doubts you have and remember that your STRIVE qualities give you an edge in terms of emotional intelligence, and spotting patterns and connections others miss.

As I write this book, we're all learning that risk-taking is unavoidable. The world is in the depths of the coronavirus pandemic, which for all its ambiguity and uncertainty, has given Sensitive Strivers the opportunity to practice embracing the unknown in everyday circumstances. Countless members of my community have commented that this time period has helped them discover strength they didn't know was possible, and what I know for sure is that the risks they're taking in the present are helping them build new levels of resourcefulness, resilience, and self-reliance. Whenever you read this book, know that you can do the same and achieve similar results. And remind yourself that risk-taking can also create unforeseen opportunities or serendipitous happy accidents that are difficult to anticipate. For example, years ago I attended a high-profile networking event to promote my business. I had just started my coaching practice, so I felt nervous about connecting to much more established business owners, but at that event I met Brian, who eventually became my fiancé.

Strategy: Try Hard Things

A *hard thing* can be something you're afraid to do because you're worried about failing or what people will think. It also includes any actions you know would be good for you, but you're avoiding or haven't made time for. My clients have put this strategy into practice by volunteering for a project even though they weren't experts or by speaking up in meetings before their ideas were totally developed. You can also try hard things outside of work, knowing that your confidence will translate. Pursuing something where you have no gauge or frame of reference for what *winning* is makes you less likely to link your self-worth to achievement. And tackling low stakes but difficult tasks is scientifically shown to improve focus, determination, and emotional resilience because without external motivators, you have to build internal strength.

Doing hard things not only makes you more likely to reach your goals, but it also:

- Gives you confidence to know you can survive fear and rejection

- Provides counter-evidence to cognitive distortions that convince you that you'll automatically fail and shows you your results could be better than you imagine

- Resets the fear center of the brain, the amygdala, to get triggered less often

As a result, your mind (and body) begins to trust that you can be *with* fear and take action *alongside of it*, even if you don't get the outcome you want. Every time you allow yourself to take a risk and experience an unpleasant emotion, you expand your capacity to tolerate discomfort and to learn to relate to it differently—with more equanimity and integrity, rather than resistance and avoidance. It may sound silly, but there's science behind this approach: Exposing yourself to stressful situations can lessen fear and avoidance by up to 90 percent. Selecting those situations *yourself*, rather than having them imposed on you by the outside world, is both empowering and builds your sense that you have what it takes to tackle future difficulties and seize opportunities. That way, when you do find yourself in unpredictable or high-pressure situations, you're already skilled at accessing your intuition and taking decisive action. At the deepest level, trying hard things helps reshape your identity. As you keep taking chances and stretching yourself, you go from viewing yourself as weak or fragile to believing that you have what it takes to rise to the occasion. You stop feeding the neural networks in your brain that whisper *you can't* and instead strengthen the ones that remind you *you can.*

Hard Things to Try

The Exercise in this chapter will help you commit to a list of hard things you'll try for yourself, but here are a few ideas to get you started.

Order a new dish for lunch

Wake up an hour early to work on a goal

Go an entire day without spending money

Send an email to someone you admire

Take a demanding hike on the weekend

Sign up for a tough obstacle race

Get Unstuck

1. HARNESS THE POWER OF *YET.* Small but mighty, *yet* helps us switch to a growth mindset and helps us acknowledge that mastery takes time. Maybe you're not attracting your ideal clients *yet*, but you can market in places they hang out. Sure, you may not feel comfortable speaking your mind in meetings *yet*, but with the right strategies, you can get there. Continue showing up and commit to learning.

2. TRY THE COFFEE CHALLENGE. The next time you go to your favorite café, Noah Kagan, founder of product marketing startup SumoMe, advises, "Go up to the counter and order coffee [or water or tea]. Then just ask for 10% off. . . . Most people will make an excuse. . . . 'Oh, I'm not afraid of doing that.' 'Oh, I don't need a discount; I have money.' But if you go ahead and ask for 10% off coffee, I guarantee that you will learn something about yourself that will surprise you."

3. REMEMBER THE 10/10/10 RULE. When the prospect of falling flat on your face seizes you, ask yourself how you'll feel about the decision to take a risk 10 weeks, 10 months, or 10 years from now. Your answers can help you put things into perspective and rally the courage you need to make the leap, whether the result of taking a risk goes right or goes wrong.

Strategy in Action: Jessica

Even before her work on the company strategy, Jessica and I had been working on trying hard things. At first, she was hesitant because she had always viewed risks as incredibly time-consuming due to her tendency to overanalyze things. I asked her to suspend her initial skepticism and instead focus on brainstorming ideas, starting with things she was laughably bad at and that had no bearing on her professional reputation. Jessica said that she couldn't draw to save her life and said jokingly that no one ever wanted to partner with her when the family played drawing games. I asked her what she could do that would be low stakes around drawing, and she said, "My friends have been asking me to go to a wine and paint night, but I'm too embarrassed." Just saying it out loud made Jessica realize that this was an obvious place to start. When she finally sat down at the easel, her painting didn't resemble the teacher's in the slightest, but she got over her nerves and even had fun with her girlfriends to boot.

In our next session, I asked Jessica to select four more hard things to try over the course of the next month—two applicable to her personal life and two to her professional life (which you'll also do in a moment in the Exercise for this chapter). On the personal side, she chose to go to a self-defense class and to take her kids to a theme park and ride a roller coaster (which she usually stayed away from). On the professional side, she accepted an invitation to be interviewed about her career on a podcast for younger Latinx professionals and did Noah Kagan's coffee challenge at the café across the street from her office. None of these things was comfortable, but after she accomplished each of them, she felt a rush and knew she was making progress toward a braver version of herself.

In the meantime, as part of her recommendations for the company's operational strategy, Jessica not only thought about the company's future, but also reflected on her own career path. She and the company had grown together, and as she imagined how it might deal with down-trending brick-and-mortar sales while making their ecommerce business more competitive, she also tried to map out her own next steps now that her life felt more balanced and she had more breathing room. It was nerve-wracking, but she realized that both she and the company might need to pivot if it was going to be successful and she was going to future-proof her career.

Later that evening as she helped her kids with their homework, Jessica had an idea. What if the company offered a clothing subscription service? It would boost online sales with recurring revenue and align with the industry trend of offering consumers more eco-friendly options. Plus, they could use their brick-and-mortar locations as pick-up and drop-off points, which would leverage their existing real estate. The concept was an instant *hell yes* for Jessica, so she knew it was worth pursuing, but she also recognized that a clothing subscription would not only be a risk for the company in terms of capital and stock price, but would also require risking her own professional reputation.

Since this wasn't an inconsequential proposal, she needed to get critical teams on her side if she was going to eventually execute the plan. She talked to her counterparts, the Chief Marketing Officer and Chief Financial Officer, and both of them thought the idea was feasible but cautioned her in a well-intentioned manner about the potential cost of presenting it to leadership. But because of the work she had done by trying hard things over the past month, Jessica felt more prepared to tolerate the fear of forging ahead, even if she didn't have all the answers and didn't know where these recommendations would take her.

Jessica pitched the concept to the CEO about two weeks later. He was skeptical at first, but because Jessica backed up her proposal with data, industry trends, and buy-in from other teams, he was willing to give Jessica a few hundred thousand dollars to run a pilot. Getting the green light on her idea was great, but Jessica mostly felt ecstatic about trusting herself. As she worked to make the clothing subscription service viable, she was mindful of working efficiently and maintaining the good habits and boundaries she had established even though times were more chaotic. She also continued to take small, low-stakes risks on a regular basis. She realized it helped her establish a deeper connection with herself in moments of fear and built up her ability to go after what she wanted without sacrificing her own ideas and needs, which translated to stepping out in her work.

MAKE BETTER DECISIONS FASTER

Taking smart risks is about making efficient decisions, but studies show that overthinking leads to slower decision-making and fewer risks. You can refer back to Chapter Five for help with conquering overthinking in general, but here's how to tackle it when it comes to risk-taking specifically:

1. PROJECT THE POTENTIAL IMPACT. It's easy to assume every decision is extremely important, that failure is just one wrong decision away, but most decisions aren't like that—they're changeable, reversible, and even if things don't work out, you've grown wiser as a result. Before you make a call, write down what priorities or people in your life will be impacted. This will help you differentiate between what's crucial and what's not worth obsessing over.

2. FOCUS ON THE KEY OBJECTIVE. Trying to weigh every possible outcome and consideration is paralyzing. To curb information overload, ask yourself, *Of the three to five possible goals I would love to meet with this single decision, which one or two will make the biggest positive impact? Of all the possible people I could please or displease, which one or two people do I least want to disappoint?*

3. GIVE YOURSELF A DEADLINE. Create accountability and creative constraints by determining a date or time by which you'll make a choice. Put it in your calendar, set a reminder on your phone, or even contact the person who is waiting for your decision and let them know when they can expect to hear from you. Leverage your Responsibility for your own benefit.

4. CREATE CONTINGENCIES. This is where your ability to see all sides of a situation comes in handy. Use an if/then formula to plan for different types of outcomes. For example, *If I find myself avoiding writing, then I will turn off Wi-Fi, take a five-minute walk to reset, or commit to writing just 100 words, no matter what they are.*

THE YES EXPERIMENT

Opening yourself up to risks will help you shift from viewing them as something to be avoided to something that's key to creating the life you want. In this Exercise, you'll devise your own version of the experiment Jessica did and commit to one month of saying yes to small risks that help you work toward a better self.

INSTRUCTIONS

1. *Select four hard things to try in the next month.* Pick two hard things that relate to your personal life outside of work and two that relate to your professional life. The things you pick should require minimal preparation and resources, but should feel like a stretch from how you currently behave day-to-day. Keep these risks simple and straightforward.

2. *Schedule them.* Limit yourself to one hard thing per week for the next month. Be wise about timing and as smart as you can be about scheduling hard things for times when your emotional/mental bandwidth is high. Don't force yourself to go to a grueling fitness class after a long, busy day where you have to work late, for example.

3. *Shift into action.* Use the tips from the "Get Unstuck" section of this chapter to work through any fear and resistance that arises in the moment.

4. *Reflect on the process.* After you complete each task, explore:

   - **How did you feel before the experience?** Focus on specific emotions, thoughts, or sensations in your body.
   - **How did you feel during the experience?** Make note of anything that shifted in your physical, mental, or emotional state.
   - **What did you learn as a result of the experience?** Include observations about your decision-making process or information about moments you shined and areas for growth.
   - **How will you carry it forward?** Even if it was difficult, what positive meaning and lessons might you draw from the experience that can influence your professional life for the better, or vice versa?

THE YES EXPERIMENT

Jessica

	WHAT I'M SAYING YES TO . . .	HOW I FELT BEFOREHAND . . .	HOW I FELT DURING . . .	
WEEK 1	*Attending the wine and paint night*	Petrified! I procrastinated getting in my car and driving there. Then, once I sat down at my easel, I nearly bolted for the door to make an escape.	At first, my mind was swirling with concerns that my friends would laugh at my painting skills. After about fifteen minutes (and a little bit of wine), I became less focused on myself and more focused on chatting with my friends and enjoying a night out.	
WEEK 2	*Riding a roller coaster at the theme park*	A mix of unsettled and happy. My kids were so excited to go to the park and have me ride with them for once, but it was unsettling to think about being flipped upside down at 60 mph.	It happened so fast that I almost didn't have time to think, which was a good thing. And actually, the experience was exhilarating. Afterwards I felt a bit queasy, but was still glad I did it. Plus, nothing can beat the smile on the kids' faces! We went on another roller coaster later in the day once my stomach settled, and I wasn't nearly as afraid as I was before the first one.	
WEEK 3	*Doing a podcast interview about my career*	One word: ugh. I don't like talking about myself. I had to get approval from HR, so as I looked over the questions the interviewer sent, I was worried that I wouldn't represent myself or the company well.	I felt like I was bragging when I spoke about what I had accomplished, but after talking about leading the brick-and-mortar expansion, I got a surge of confidence. On the flip side, it's always difficult to talk about mistakes, but telling someone else about them made me realize I had overcome a lot.	
WEEK 4	*Trying the Coffee Challenge at the café across the street from the office*	When Melody first told me about this, I cringed and had a deep reaction of disgust ("You want me to try *what*?").	When I asked the cashier for 10% off my latte, she looked at me sideways and then went to get her manager. I felt my entire body sweat.	

WHAT I LEARNED . . .	HOW I'LL CARRY THIS FORWARD . . .
1. I can find enjoyment in an activity even if I'm not the best at it. I typically place a high value on achievement, but the wine and paint night reinforced the value of connection and simply being present with people I care about. 2. Everyone is more focused on themselves than they are on me. Being my own worst critic is wasted energy.	1. This has prompted me to think about taking my boundary and values work even deeper by looking for ways I can optimize for presence and connection in my life, especially at home. 2. Typically, when I speak at leadership meetings, I am so concerned that the CEO and other execs are analyzing my every word. In reality, they are in their own heads, and there's not as much risk to putting my ideas forth as I may perceive.
I can face my fears. I walked away with a sense of pride. I also learned that sometimes situations are beyond my control and happen quickly, but I can still handle it and appreciate the ride.	At work right now, there are many situations that are beyond my control, so it's good practice functioning with things happening at light speed around me. It's clear to me now that conquering my fears gets easier with repetition, which is a principle I'll need to call on as I put together the operational plan at work.
I'm thrilled to be an example to young professionals, and I didn't realize that that mattered to me. Just because I haven't done everything perfectly doesn't mean I'm not a role model.	I've always worked behind the scenes at my company, but maybe I should consider increasing my visibility industry wide. Company executives speak on business podcasts all the time, so next time the opportunity arises I'm going to volunteer.
The manager said giving discounts was against store policy, but you know what? I didn't care, because I DID IT! And I didn't undermine myself by dismissing my request. I stood strong, smiled, and said, "Thanks, anyway!" That was a huge moment of strength and a demonstration of how far I've come in valuing myself.	Asking for more! Throughout my career, I've simply accepted what's been given to me and asked for *just enough*. This has shown me that there's no harm in trying because the worst I may hear is *no*, and I can bounce back.

THE YES EXPERIMENT

	WHAT I'M SAYING YES TO . . .	HOW I FELT BEFOREHAND . . .	HOW I FELT DURING . . .	
WEEK 1				
WEEK 2				
WEEK 3				
WEEK 4				

	WHAT I LEARNED . . .	HOW I'LL CARRY THIS FORWARD . . .

SPEAK UP AND
STAND YOUR GROUND

12

"When I'm trusting and being myself as full as possible, everything in my life reflects this by falling into place easily, often miraculously."

—SHAKTI GAWAIN

AS SHE HEADED INTO THE SUMMER, KATHERINE, from Chapter Eight, continued to blossom. She had used her new manager course to rethink her approach to how she worked with her team and had met several other new managers whom she consulted for ideas and advice. Through our coaching, she was more in control of her Emotionality and able to focus on her own advancement. One skill Katherine had incorporated into her regular routine was recognizing and praising others—Mark included—and she had noticed a shift in his attitude as a result even though he occasionally still made snarky comments in meetings.

Her efforts on the workplace culture committee were also taking off. Katherine had been instrumental in creating a beautifully designed company welcome kit for onboarding new employees, which had given her greater exposure to the CEO and more visibility overall. Katherine's work positioned her as a mentor for junior employees—as a leader who was skilled at inspiring others and bringing them together. It also gave her faith that she could tackle unexpected challenges as they arose.

Now, Katherine was getting ready for mid-year performance reviews, which meant she would receive a review from Beth and that she had to give one to Mark. These discussions had always made her nervous before, but Beth was an extremely supportive supervisor, and she knew this would force her to have the conversation with Mark about his overall attitude. For her own review, Katherine prepared a list of accomplishments. During her review, Beth noted that Katherine had grown over the past six months and that Beth was proud of how quickly Katherine was stepping up into new responsibilities. On her self-evaluation, Katherine reported that one area for improvement was handling difficult personalities, namely Mark. Beth asked her if she had ever spoken to him about the website launch last year. Katherine explained that she planned to talk to him about his overall behavior during his review because only the day before, Mark had left the names of other team members off a report. Even though he had done much of the work, members of the product team had helped significantly and deserved credit. Beth agreed that it was now or never.

Katherine realized that part of her role as his manager would be to keep Mark on board while simultaneously telling him that he needed to improve his people skills and his efforts at collaboration. Katherine suspected that his review might be challenging, but her conversation with Beth made her realize that being more assertive was critical to her own growth and advancement. While Katherine felt a familiar surge of Emotionality imagining all the different outcomes of the review, she was able to recognize herself getting upset, to rein it in, and to use it instead to fuel her determination to diplomatically manage the situation with Mark.

Just like Katherine, throughout this book, you've examined how you've felt and behaved in the past and have decided how you can approach the world differently and reveal more of who you are. You have to be able to state your opinions and use your voice alongside the unpredictability of the workplace and other people. Up until now, you may have considered speaking your mind or asserting your feelings, needs, or beliefs as mean or unpleasant. But being assertive is a way to stand your ground and say what you think with both conviction and compassion. One of the most critical shifts you can make is a change in mindset from believing that assertiveness is aggressive to living in a way in which articulating your goals, boundaries, and needs is second nature.

In my work, assertiveness stands out as the number one skill that demonstrates confidence to the outside world and helps you cultivate a life that supports your ambitions and inner self. Whether you're asking for a raise or new opportunity, managing up, or setting limits with family and friends, you have to know how to get your voice heard with tact and professionalism. Most of all, it's important you learn to communicate with strength in a way that leverages the innate warmth, caring, and concern of your STRIVE qualities.

Express Your Truth

Being assertive is all about finding the middle ground between the two extremes of aggressive and passive communication. It involves:

- **Standing your ground.** Projecting confidence, taking up space, and pushing back when you need to requires that you value yourself enough to put forth your ideas, even at the risk that others won't like them.

- **Approaching situations with objectivity and respect for others' viewpoints.** Speaking up for yourself clearly and concisely means that you can work through disagreements in a low-stress, no-drama way that keeps your Emotionality and Thoughtfulness well balanced.

- **Finding win-wins where possible.** Act with integrity and in accordance with your values, regardless of whether you get your way or not.

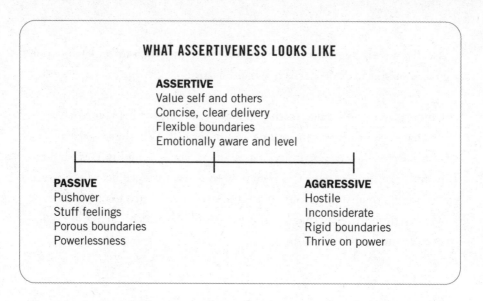

WHAT ASSERTIVENESS LOOKS LIKE

ASSERTIVE
Value self and others
Concise, clear delivery
Flexible boundaries
Emotionally aware and level

PASSIVE
Pushover
Stuff feelings
Porous boundaries
Powerlessness

AGGRESSIVE
Hostile
Inconsiderate
Rigid boundaries
Thrive on power

GETTING THE TEAM TO BUY IN TO YOUR IDEAS

Passive: Wait for someone else to make the first suggestion, then simply agree, rather than offer other ideas.

Aggressive: Present your idea as the one the team must adopt and, without taking a breath, assign tasks.

Assertive: Acknowledge the strong points colleagues have suggested and add your perspective, backed up by facts.

REBOUNDING AFTER BEING DENIED A RAISE

Passive: Swallow your disappointment and utter, *Oh, that's fine*, but then go home and vent about it.

Aggressive: Inform your boss that you're going to begin looking for a job where you'll be treated better.

Assertive: Define tangible goals and targets that you can review when you revisit your salary request down the road.

MANAGING A DIRECT REPORT WHO'S UNDERPERFORMING

Passive: Stay up until 2 a.m. correcting their mistakes—and don't mention anything in your next one-on-one.

Aggressive: Go full-on Jerry Maguire on them, demanding to know why they're so incompetent.

Assertive: State their work isn't acceptable and say you want to help them overcome roadblocks to meeting requirements.

In the same way that you're trying to balance your STRIVE qualities, you're trying to balance yourself on the seesaw of assertive communication. Once you find that happy medium, being assertive opens you up to new and better opportunities. Beyond boosting your self-esteem and helping you avoid burnout, assertiveness can also earn you respect, influence, and greater authority—all of which can lead to career advancement and a higher quality of life. Plus, every time you take the brave step to speak up, you're setting an example to create a culture of psychological safety and accountability where others feel empowered to voice their opinions without fear of retribution.

Strategy: Perfect the Communication Trifecta

Speaking and acting with assertiveness takes practice, awareness, and regular readjusting, but once you find the balance that works for you, you take another step toward commanding respect in almost any situation. Here's a three-part model you can use to deliver your message calmly, clearly, and straightforwardly:

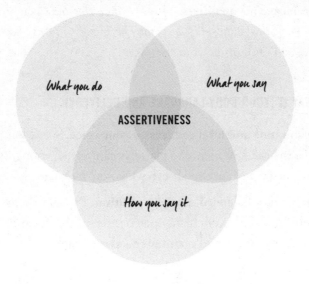

WHAT YOU DO (THE ACTIONS YOU TAKE)

- **Take initiative.** Address problems before they get out of hand and offer forward-looking solutions.

- **Make explicit requests.** State what you want, ask for what you need, and don't expect others to read your mind.

- **Listen with an open mind.** Summarize and clarify to check your understanding (i.e., *What I hear you saying is . . .* and *Is that right?*).

- **Praise and highlight positive behaviors.** Remember to tell people what they're doing right and notice when things are going well.

WHAT YOU SAY (THE CONTENT OF YOUR MESSAGE)

- **Write down five key points in advance.** Write down headlines that represent the progression of the conversation you want to have to guide it without scripting it word-for-word.

- **Take ownership.** Use first-person *I* statements like, *I feel unappreciated when . . .* , *My reaction was one of . . .* , and *What I thought was . . .*

- **Speak definitively and concisely.** Fewer words strengthen your message, so lead with your main point and trim away excess detail or unnecessary explanation.

- **Drop prefaces and qualifiers.** Phrases like, *This may not be important, but . . .* , *I know this sounds silly . . .* , *I may be wrong . . .* , and *I hope you won't be upset . . .* all undermine your message.

HOW YOU SAY IT (YOUR BODY LANGUAGE AND DELIVERY)

- **Keep a calm tone and level cadence to your voice.** Speak loudly enough for people to hear. Use silence to pause, organize your thoughts, and give the other person a chance to absorb what you're saying and respond.

- **Stand or sit in a balanced, upright position.** Pretend there is a string above your head, hold your arms open or relaxed downward (no crossed arms or hair twirling), and maintain good eye contact.

- **Be attuned to what's happening.** Watch for changes in the other person's body language and look for inconsistencies. For example, does the person seem surprised by what you're saying? Or are they telling you yes while shaking their head no?

- **Make wise choices around context.** Consider the time of day and medium through which you choose to deliver the message (i.e., email, face-to-face, phone, direct messaging).

At its core, assertiveness is about respecting yourself enough to trust your intuition and to live your life accordingly. Every time you're willing to express what's important to you, you reinforce to your brain that your wishes are important and valuable.

Get Unstuck

1. TRY AND TRY AGAIN. Your words may not come out right the first time, the timing might be off, or you may feel paralyzed when trying to speak your mind. All is not lost. Follow up with an email restating your ideas, ask to have a conversation after you gather your thoughts, or seize another chance to contribute.

2. PICK YOUR BATTLES AND ADJUST YOUR STYLE. Give someone the benefit of the doubt once or twice, but if the behavior becomes a pattern, speak up. Adjust your style depending on your counterpart. You may have to veer slightly toward the aggressive side if you're dealing with someone who is rude and hostile, and veer a little more toward the passive, deferential side if you're speaking with a higher-up.

3. TAKE A MINUTE TO THINK. If things get heated during a conversation, ask for time to process. For example, *I value our working relationship and want to make sure I give you the best response possible. Can we put this on the agenda for our meeting next week?*

4. ADDRESS CRYING COURAGEOUSLY. It's better to acknowledge your reaction than try to hide it. Say something like, *As you can see, I'm feeling pretty invested in this, which is why I'm having an emotional reaction.*

Say It Like a Boss

INSTEAD OF . . .		TRY . . .
You always dump things on me last minute.	→	I feel overwhelmed when you ask for materials three hours before the deadline.
Yes, I can do that!	→	I hear this is important. Let's look at my priorities and see what can shift or be eliminated.
Could you please cover the meeting?	→	I need you to cover the meeting.
Would it be okay to move forward?	→	I'll move forward unless otherwise specified.
Just wanted to check in.	→	I'd like an update by the end of the day.
Ugh, I'm so sorry for missing that!	→	Nice catch! Thank you for spotting that.
Hopefully this makes sense?	→	What questions do you have?
I'm rambling again.	→	I'm a verbal processor and appreciate you letting me talk this through.

Strategy in Action: Katherine

In our next coaching session, Katherine and I strategized how she could assertively deliver feedback to Mark in his performance review using the Communication Trifecta. But before we talked tactics, we needed to address her mindset. At first, Katherine was concerned that criticizing Mark would lead him to retaliate by underperforming, but through our discussion she came to understand that withholding the feedback would be worse and would actually be unfair to Mark. She hadn't been clear before about her expectations and the potential consequences, and she knew that if she didn't tell him now and if he didn't change his behavior, it would negatively impact the whole team.

As we talked about the What You Do piece of delivering her message, Katherine realized she needed to reschedule Mark's performance review so that it wasn't before an important meeting they had about their ongoing work with the team's biggest and most important client. She didn't want them to be rushed, and she also knew that both she and Mark might need time to process their conversation. At the end of her email rescheduling their discussion, Katherine said she was looking forward to talking about his accomplishments and his areas for growth, so there were no surprises.

In terms of What You Say, Katherine wanted to set a positive tone, so she created a bulleted list to stay on track. When she and Mark sat down, they spent about twenty minutes talking about Mark's achievements during which Katherine referred to her notes, praised Mark, and highlighted all the ways he had contributed to the team, before segueing into a discussion of his weaknesses. She prefaced it by saying, "As your manager, it's important for me to point out areas where you can build your skills and grow professionally. That's why I want to share feedback that may be hard to hear, but will help you improve. I also want to get your point of view and work together on an action plan." Katherine acknowledged that her being passive in the past may have contributed to the tension, so she added, "We can also talk about how I may have contributed to this problem and how I can support you better."

Next, Katherine laid out two key areas of growth for Mark—interpersonal communication and collaboration. Katherine began by describing why both areas were crucial to their teamwork and important to the company. After laying out what each competency entailed, Katherine transitioned to specifics and brought up the situation that had happened a few days ago, saying, "When I saw the report, I noticed it only had your name on it. From now on, I'd like you to add a checkpoint to your process to make sure that everyone is acknowledged for their work."

After she finished, Katherine shifted into listener mode. She asked Mark, "What do you make of the feedback I shared?"

Mark crossed his arms, leaned back in his chair, and scowled. "You know, I'm not happy. I really don't think what you've said is fair."

In the past, Katherine might have tried to roll back some of her comments while stuttering or tripping over her words, but this time was different. She was able to stick to her guns and reassert her authority, saying, "I can understand why you're upset, but part of my responsibility is to evaluate each team member's performance to the best of my ability and point out where I see opportunities for improvement. So, while I know it's a drag to hear criticism, I still need you to meet the performance expectations I outlined. We can shift to talking about a plan for making that possible."

Mark scoffed and looked away while Katherine kept her gaze on him and waited for a response. After thirty seconds of silence, Mark muttered that he would need some time to think about the plan. Executing the steps we talked about, Katherine said in a calm voice that she understood and asked him to bring ideas to their next one-on-one. Then, Mark walked out of the room, letting the door slam behind him. Katherine let out a huge sigh of relief. Even though the situation wasn't resolved yet and she didn't know whether or not they would reach a compromise, she felt proud of herself for having kept calm in a tense situation and for having used strategies that allowed her to stand her ground. She knew that with this accomplishment behind her, she would go into the next situation like this with more confidence. After all, conflict was inevitable, but she didn't have to dread it every time.

Speak Up Shortcuts

HUMBLE BRAG

○ **Send a monthly round-up of your and/or your team's key accomplishments.** Focus on numbers that quantify your achievements and social proof in the form of testimonials or other praise.

○ **Add an "Accomplishments" section to your one-on-one agenda with your manager.** And if you're a leader, start team meetings by having everyone share one win from the past week.

○ **Create a brain trust.** Follow up with a mentor to let them know how you implemented their advice, or find a work friend who can toot your horn and who you can help shine in return.

○ **Showcase your expertise.** Offer to host a lunch-and-learn for other staff members or train a new team member.

CONTRIBUTE IN MEETINGS

○ **Arrive early.** Use the extra time to build rapport and warm up by making low-key conversation.

○ **Speak up within the first ten minutes.** Once you contribute one thought or idea, you'll feel more relaxed and positive.

○ **Use the PREP framework**. Make a *point* succinctly, back it up with a *reason*, provide *evidence*, and end by reiterating your *point*.

○ **Ask questions that spark further discussions.** For example, you could say, *What's a reasonable timeline? How would we like to approach this?*

SAY NO, KINDLY

○ **Put space between the request and your acceptance.** Before committing, say, *I have to think about it, Let me check my calendar,* or *Let's first talk about how we might make that work.*

○ **Offer an alternative.** If a deadline is unreasonable, say, *I'm happy to do this. Realistically, here's what I can do in this time frame,* or *Here are the resources I'll need to make this happen.*

○ **Replace apology with gratitude.** *I'm sorry I can't do that* becomes *Thank you for thinking of me.*

○ **Explain how someone can hire or pay you.** Try, *My work schedule is packed and lunch/coffee isn't possible, but I could see us working together on this* or *I'd love to work together and help you solve this problem. Let's discuss a package that makes sense.*

ASK FOR A RAISE OR PROMOTION

○ **Plant the seed.** Mention your goal to your manager early on by saying, *While my first priority is to excel in my current role, my long-term goal is to advance and I'd like your support to set myself up for success.*

○ **Anticipate needs and proactively problem solve.** Know what your manager's key priorities are. Seek out stretch assignments where you can make an impact.

○ **Showcase your past accomplishments *and* your future plans.** Your manager wants to know how paying you more or promoting you will result in ROI (return on investment) for the company.

○ **Be prepared to hear no.** Rejection isn't the end of a negotiation. Find out what goals you need to hit to earn a salary adjustment.

RECEIVE FEEDBACK GRACEFULLY

○ **Don't immediately strategize a defense.** Even if your initial response is hurt or anger, take a deep breath, thank the person for their input, and ask for specific examples.

○ **Come prepared with questions of your own.** *What is working well?* and *What two suggestions do you have for what I should try next time?* are my favorites.

○ **Request time to process the feedback.** In the moment when you get tough feedback, you can say, *I appreciate hearing your concerns. I'd like to collect my thoughts so that I can give you the best response possible. Can we loop back next week?*

○ **Make sense of it.** Break feedback into three buckets: 1. What they *said* (exact words, without adding interpretation), 2. What's *wrong* with the feedback (to vent your frustrations), and 3. What might be *right* with it (so you don't lose the value of what they're saying).

CONFRONT WITH CONFIDENCE

Many will view your newfound ability to effectively speak up for yourself as positive, but some people may become upset or angry, especially if you used to be overly accommodating. In this Exercise, you'll practice responding when your audience isn't receptive.

INSTRUCTIONS

1. *Identify a conversation you need to have.* The situation may be relevant to one of your boundaries being crossed, a value you have, or a goal that's important to you.

2. *Outline What You Do, What You Say, and How You Say It.* You won't always be able to prepare in advance, but do so where possible.

3. *Have the conversation!* Muster your courage and make it happen.

4. *Respond to pushback.* Pick *one* of the following techniques to try when and if the conversation gets heated.

   - **Active listening.** Validate the other person and attempt to understand their viewpoint. Do this by restating, *It sounds to me like you're unhappy with how the meeting went. Am I correct?* Or, posing open-ended questions such as, *What's your reaction to what I've said? How can I support you?*

   - **Aim for a workable compromise.** Offer an alternative proposal or solution, such as, *How can we meet in the middle? How can we get to a number that works for both of us?*

   - **Use silence.** Pause three to five seconds before responding to stonewall aggression, like Katherine did with Mark.

   - **Try the broken record technique.** Repeat one phrase in an even-handed tone, such as *I'm speaking, That's not relevant*, or *Please don't speak to me that way.*

5. *Reflect.* After the interaction, explore what went well and what didn't and how you can improve your approach going forward.

CONFRONT WITH CONFIDENCE
Katherine

WHAT YOU DO

OLD BEHAVIORS	NEW BEHAVIORS
Travel on the same day as Mark's review	Reschedule Mark's review so we aren't rushed
Avoid bringing up how he left the team's names off the report	Highlight Mark's contributions
	Send him an agenda beforehand so there are no surprises

WHAT YOU SAY

OLD BEHAVIORS	NEW BEHAVIORS
"I'm rambling."	"You're an asset to the team."
"Am I making sense?"	"What's your take on what I shared?"
"I'm sorry for giving you this feedback."	Use silence if he gets upset

HOW YOU SAY IT

OLD BEHAVIORS	NEW BEHAVIORS
Slouched over	Sit up straight, pretending there's a board against my back
Ducking eye contact	Position myself more side-by-side with him versus across the table

CONVERSATION OUTLINE

INTRODUCTION
- I want this to be a two-way conversation.

MAIN POINTS
- Highlight accomplishments re: client project last year.
- Two key areas for improvement: interpersonal communication and collaboration.
- Example: leaving names off the materials.
- I felt concerned and disappointed.

CONCLUSION
- In the future, I need you to be mindful about giving everyone credit.
- As your manager, I'm here to give you honest feedback and help you create a plan.

CONFRONT WITH CONFIDENCE

On the dotted lines, note the behaviors you don't want to do. Use the full lines to write down ones you do.

WHAT YOU DO

OLD BEHAVIORS

NEW BEHAVIORS

WHAT YOU SAY

OLD BEHAVIORS

NEW BEHAVIORS

HOW YOU SAY IT

OLD BEHAVIORS

NEW BEHAVIORS

CONVERSATION OUTLINE

INTRODUCTION

MAIN POINTS

CONCLUSION

BOUNCE BACK FROM SETBACKS

13

"Calm seas are where you'll find peace,
but storms are where you'll find your power."

—JILL WINTERSTEEN

IN THE WEEKS LEADING UP TO THE KEYNOTE, Cassie, from Chapter Five, had high hopes that her performance would catapult her into the next phase of growth within the company. She built a great deck and wrote a brand-new speech she was proud of. She rehearsed in front of a few trusted colleagues and used their feedback to revise her presentation and to anticipate questions that might come from the audience. Most importantly, she practiced speaking concisely so that she could put her concerns about that one piece of feedback to rest. On the day of the conference, she looked out across the room, took a breath, and began her talk. Her preparation and poise showed in every word, and at the end of the day Greg told her she was a shoo-in for a promotion. Cassie was elated.

Once the promotion went into effect about six weeks later, Cassie handed off the recruitment of junior talent so she could focus on bringing in executive leaders, which was both higher stakes and higher-impact work. Cassie jumped into her new assignment with vigor. While the tasks were challenging, she felt these new duties leveraged her relationship-building skills and her knack for reading people. Two months later, Cassie was ready to make an offer to her first candidate—a potential VP of Business Development. Cassie had spent weeks organizing internal interviews and meetings for the candidate, who had signaled that if the company made an offer, he would accept. Cassie had felt so sure that the candidate was a good fit that she had lobbied for a salary offer tens of thousands of dollars above the candidate's asking amount.

Cassie was practically giddy when she picked up the phone to make the offer. The first sign of trouble came when the candidate seemed less than thrilled to hear from her. The offer call lasted just five minutes, but Cassie told herself that she must have caught him at a bad time. It was only the next morning when she got an email from the candidate declining the offer that Cassie's heart sank. Even though she called and emailed the candidate over the course of the next week, she got no answer, and she eventually had to tell Greg and the senior leadership team that they would have to begin their search again. Cassie was proud that her sense of panic at having missed the mark on her first executive recruit was not as intense as it might have been several months before, but she still felt demoralized by how the prospective hire had left her in the lurch.

Later that week, Cassie found herself slowly putting together a revised list of potential candidates when her wife called from the emergency room. She had slipped on water in the bathroom and had broken her foot. Cassie raced to the hospital, where she found her wife in good spirits, but with a huge cast on her foot. She would have to keep the cast on for four weeks and then use a walking cast for four weeks after that. She couldn't drive, which meant that she was going to need help getting to work and pitching in on her share of the household chores. Cassie took the rest of the week off to take care of her wife, but in the evenings, she stayed up late trying to get the recruiting plan back on track even though she felt exhausted and far less motivated than usual. By Monday morning, she was staring down a string of emails asking for an update while escorting her wife to a doctor's appointment where the doctor emphasized that her wife needed to stay off her feet.

The whole situation sent Cassie into a tailspin. She wasn't achieving as much in her new role as she had hoped, *and* her obligations at home had just gone through the roof. In spite of reining in her overthinking, she felt helpless and frustrated in a way that she hadn't experienced in a very long time as she faced down what felt like huge roadblocks ahead.

Whether at home or work, setbacks can derail you and lead you to feel like you're backsliding on the progress you've made throughout this book. But fear not—you can apply the tools you've already learned in flexible and creative ways to address setbacks at the source, whether they're small or large, internal or external. By reaffirming your commitment to yourself and leveraging the best of your STRIVE qualities, you can handle any curveball that comes your way.

A Stumble Is Not a Fall

While setbacks are difficult for everyone, your biology and psychology as a Sensitive Striver leave you particularly affected by the inner turmoil that typically accompanies unanticipated and challenging situations like:

- A gap between expectations and reality
- A loss of motivation
- An illness or health problem
- Emotional exhaustion due to the busy pace of work and life
- Letting boundaries slip and taking on too much

As you've realized throughout this book, in order to thrive, you'll need to actively manage your STRIVE qualities, and nowhere is this more important than when it comes to rebounding from setbacks. Once you accept that you need a specialized framework for interpreting, processing, and moving forward from setbacks, everything will become easier. After all, working toward your ambitions and achieving greatness is *supposed* to be hard. As you take more risks, assert yourself, and continue charting your own course toward success, you'll inevitably bump up against adversity. The bigger you play, and the more chances you take, the more you need to be prepared for low periods, but part of owning your progress is taking full responsibility for lifting yourself out of a funk when it occurs. The good news is that you can do this by calling on the skills you've already learned and synthesizing them.

Before we go on, let me make something clear: Setbacks are not the same as failing, even though for much of your life up until now, you may have equated one with the other. Failure happens when you throw in the towel and give up, when there are no other options. Setbacks are temporary derailments, but do not extinguish the persistence and commitment you carry with you. When handled effectively, they can be transformed into a launching pad.

WHEN THE GOING GETS TOUGH

Because this book is focused on helping you achieve long-term change and lasting balance, it's important to mention that at some point you may feel like you're not getting anywhere, or that you were making a lot of progress, but now you're stalled. You could also be thrust into difficult situations that are beyond your control, like the global COVID-19 pandemic.

When you're learning to trust yourself, it's scientifically proven that you *will* hit low points. Not only is this okay, it's normal, because of the phenomenon of the change curve. You may be familiar with this idea from management or business training, but it applies to your development as a Sensitive Striver, too. On the vertical axis is well-being (motivation, happiness, productivity, etc.), and the other axis represents time. As you begin to transform yourself using the tools in this book, you may find your motivation temporarily drops. Why? Change is hard! Plus, your energy is a fluctuating resource, and the fact is that things *will* happen that rock your confidence, enthusiasm, and focus. Anything worth doing comes with a plunge where doubt and confusion set in, and nothing is more worth doing than becoming the person you want to be.

Even though the change curve is an expected part of the journey, it's also the most stressful and unpleasant part. As a Sensitive Striver, you're especially susceptible to feeling angry at yourself or annoyed that you're not moving faster. You may be more irritable, skeptical, or even sad and slightly listless because you're unsure how long this period will last. If you're experiencing disillusionment or disappointment that you're backtracking, you may be in Stage 3 of the curve. But it also means you're on to something. Many people quit while in the depths of the change valley, but what my clients discover is that seeing through the hard times eventually gives way to strength, growth, and new opportunity.

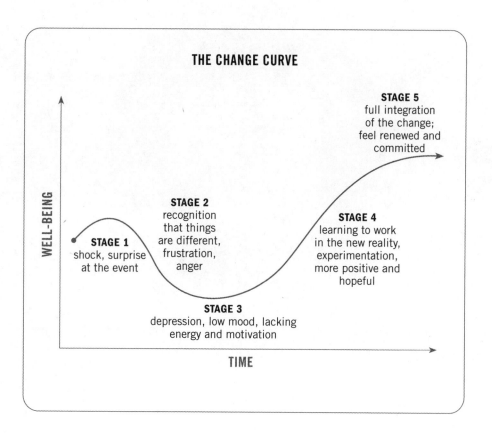

THE CHANGE CURVE

STAGE 5
full integration
of the change;
feel renewed and
committed

STAGE 2
recognition
that things
are different,
frustration,
anger

STAGE 4
learning to work
in the new reality,
experimentation,
more positive and
hopeful

STAGE 1
shock, surprise
at the event

STAGE 3
depression, low mood, lacking
energy and motivation

WELL-BEING

TIME

Strategy: Begin Again

All Sensitive Strivers get thrown into the change curve for one reason or another, especially as you rise to new levels in your life or encounter unexpected obstacles. But when you're able to recognize what's happening and be deliberate with your actions, setbacks don't have to be as painful. Coming out on the other side ready to recommit to your path requires that you harness all the skills you have learned throughout this book and apply them to rest, reflect, recalibrate, and then get back on track. Use the following checklist to thrive through slumps rather than suffer through them.

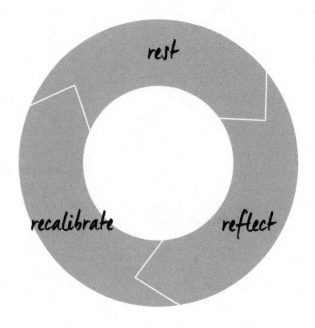

REST

It's one thing to say low points can be a positive thing, and another to believe it. You can't begin to recover from the negative feelings a setback inflicts until you gain distance from the situation, so the first stage is to take time off from the problem. Doing so allows your nervous system to settle and for you to adjust your perspective.

_____ **Ground yourself.** Revisit the tools and techniques you've learned to find your center and integrate your emotions without letting them take over your reactions and behaviors (Chapter Four). Allow yourself to feel the hurt, disappointment, and embarrassment that may come from a setback. You don't need to focus on finding the silver lining just yet.

_____ **Manage your thoughts.** Even if you're unsure how long the setback will last, keeping a thought journal (Chapter Five) will help you stop destructive self-talk in its tracks. Instead of seeing this moment as the end of your story, imagine it as an event in the middle of your journey. What would you like to come next? What could happen in the future that would reveal this dip to be a neutral or even pivotal point in becoming the hero of your own story?

REFLECT

You've come a long way since you first picked up this book. Now is the time to remember that you can do hard things, and to remind yourself why you picked up this book in the first place: to go from self-sabotage to self-trust. Make a list of your successes and use the inner strength and self-confidence you've built to carry you through this slump and to the other side.

_____ **Revise your permission slip.** Give yourself permission to try things over and over again, including permission to make mistakes, take breaks, or be less than 100 percent productive. There's no better time to revisit your permission slip (Chapter Three) than now because you'll need it to let go of preconceived notions of how things ought to work out and embrace starting again.

_____ **Consult your intuition.** Call on the discernment you've developed through this journey to assess the information you have, to accept that there will always be unknowns, and to trust your gut to decide what is best for you in the moment, even if it feels as if it may not bring immediate results (Chapter Six).

_____ **Remember your core values.** Hold fast to the core values you've defined (Chapter Eight) and let them be your guide. Maybe the way you've expressed them didn't quite work out this time, but setbacks don't mean that you have to change the essence of who you are. Look for new ways to take action on your values to bring your STRIVE qualities into greater balance.

RECALIBRATE

You can still stay committed to your outcome while becoming more flexible in your approach. As you've reflected, perhaps you've noticed what is or is not working. With that insight, take one step forward. That step may simply mean being still, because you don't always need to be pushing and forcing. You now have the wherewithal to make an informed decision about how to respond in a way that serves you and matches what matters to you the most.

_____ **Recommit to (or reset) your goals.** Now that you're deep into the change curve, you may need to reexamine the goals you set for yourself based on unanticipated information, events, or feedback. Update or create new goals using the Commit, Challenge, Crush It framework (Chapter Nine) to accommodate the changing situation.

_____ **Bolster or rebuild your boundaries.** Decide how your boundaries (Chapter Seven) have to shift or change. Do you need to reassert boundaries that were working for you but that you accidentally let down? Would other boundaries now better suit your situation? Remember that boundaries don't exist to keep other people at bay, but rather to preserve your energy by creating sustainable, supportive limits.

_____ **Change the game.** If you've defined what you thought you wanted, but it didn't quite go the way you had planned—maybe you took on new responsibilities at work, but they weren't a good fit or maybe you tried joining a co-working space that was too chaotic—adjust and try again. Or use the self-knowledge you've gained to make a different choice altogether that is a better fit between your personality and your professional life (Chapter Ten).

Even though these stages are designed to help make setbacks shorter and hurt less, coming back strong may take longer than you like, so you'll have to be patient with yourself and the conditions you're in. You can't wipe out decades of habitual thinking and behavior in a short time, even with the best intentions, nor can you control all of the ambiguity and uncertainty inherent in the world. But, you can rely on this process and repeat it as many times as needed until you emerge on the other side.

Get Unstuck

1. TAKE A MOMENT TO HALT. When you feel yourself spiraling down ask yourself: *Am I hungry, angry, lonely, or tired?* Then meet the need. Grab a snack, phone a friend, or take a quick nap. As a Sensitive Striver, you are more susceptible to energy shifts, and if your nervous system is depleted, your response will be more intense.

2. GET OUTSIDE OF YOURSELF. Buy a coffee for the person behind you in line or carry groceries for an elderly neighbor. You can also try an awe walk—a walking meditation where you focus on getting outside of your own head and into the world.

3. MAKE A LIST OF WHAT YOU'VE LEARNED. What would you do differently if you were to make a repeat attempt? Those shoulda-woulda-couldas aren't lingering in the past—they're all lessons you've learned from the stumble.

Strategy in Action: Cassie

In our next meeting, Cassie was clearly stressed. She had spent the week going into the office early to look for another VP candidate, and rushing out before she was finished with her own assignments to pick up her wife from work. Once Cassie was home, she had to clean, cook, do laundry, and manage all the other household tasks that came up. Her wife was getting better, but they still had six more weeks of this ahead of them, and Cassie felt a desire to get back on an upswing both at home and at work.

As we talked about each situation, Cassie knew that no one blamed her personally for the fact that the company's first-choice candidate hadn't taken the job. Greg had even pointed out that executive recruiting was far more complex than her previous tasks and said that she would learn how to navigate it over time. As Cassie looked at her calendar and thought about her schedule, she was worried she had anything but time, and she felt surges of panic, wondering if she could handle it all.

Cassie's goal in our coaching session was to shake the funk she was in and to reconnect with the excitement and sense of possibility she felt when she first got the promotion. Another priority was to be present and supportive for her wife, but she realized pretty quickly that with the pressure she was under, she had abandoned some of her good habits and had started overfunctioning and letting her overthinking send her back to a negative place.

I introduced the idea of beginning again to Cassie, and we made a plan for the next week. Her first priority was to get some rest to make space for the work ahead. That weekend, she slept in, ordered takeout, and committed to a digital detox to clear her head. With a few nights of sleep and some reflection, she could see more clearly that what she'd been doing during the past two weeks wasn't sustainable. She had always prided herself on being able to manage any situation, but once she looked at the whole picture, she saw that she needed to give herself permission *not* to do it all alone and to ask for help.

To recalibrate, Cassie and her wife called her mother-in-law to help with getting Cassie's wife home every day so that Cassie could have time and space to conduct the executive search without rushing out the door. They also committed to paying for grocery and laundry services, and agreed that they would order dinner several times a week to make cooking and cleaning easier on both of them. While Cassie may have refused the help before, she knew that she couldn't satisfy her core values of Focus and Humility without it.

She was also ready to learn from the recruiting situation. On Wednesday, she and Greg had a postmortem to debrief on what happened with losing the candidate, and from that meeting, Cassie developed a plan to improve her candidate sourcing procedures. She also set a boundary that she would not take a candidate's decisions personally going forward and knew that she needed someone besides Greg to talk to when things didn't go right. Once her wife's foot healed, Cassie joined an HR Women in Leadership organization to get more support with discussing issues at work and approaches to dealing with them.

Now a year into the role, Cassie has found her groove. After the initial rejection, she ended up hiring the next candidate, who turned out to be a great fit for the organization. Even though she has had other minor missteps, she is now able to shake setbacks—internal or external—because each time, she revisits the tools she learned to keep her STRIVE qualities balanced. Cassie even went so far as to keep a log of "areas for growth" on her computer so that she could keep track of lessons learned and reflect back on all that she had overcome.

Speak Up Shortcuts

Most of the time the ruts you'll face are due to the natural ebbs and flows of motivation and life. But every once in a while, you may genuinely mess up. Here is how to make amends when you make a mistake.

○ **Don't exaggerate.** With few exceptions—like if you're a pilot or surgeon—work gaffes aren't life-and-death and can be resolved or corrected. Be kind to yourself and pull out the positive self-talk: *People make mistakes—I guess it was my turn. It's embarrassing, and I'll get through it.*

○ **Own up to it.** Apologize if you need to, but don't overdo it. A swift *I made an error and I'm working on fixing it ASAP* is usually enough to save face and your reputation.

○ **Patch relationships.** If the mistake affected other people, you may need to rebuild trust. A good rule of thumb is that it takes five positive interactions to outweigh one negative one.

○ **Make adjustments.** Evaluate how and why the slipup happened and create a plan for what you can do to prevent it going forward. For example, one of my clients was mortified that she kept misspelling an important client's name and she was worried it would jeopardize the account. She typed out a list of her clients and stuck it to her cubicle for the reminder and easy reference.

○ **Find a healthy distraction.** Give yourself permission to take your mind off the mistake. Diffuse dwelling by getting lost in a work project you enjoy or taking a cuddle break with your pet.

YOUR NEXT HORIZON

Balancing your STRIVE qualities is an ongoing journey, which means that set-backs give you the chance to assess the next horizon for your growth. Even if you feel that by now most of the time you're well balanced, this final Exercise will help you evaluate how to continue bettering yourself.

INSTRUCTIONS

1. *Bring to mind a setback.* Recall a slump (brief or ongoing) you've hit since you last filled out your Wheel of Balance in Chapter Eight. Consider the emotions you felt, what you thought, and how you reacted. Complete your third Wheel of Balance with this situation in mind.

2. *Take note of your accomplishments.* Place this Wheel of Balance side-by-side with the first one you completed in Chapter One and the second from Chapter Eight. Take in the positive changes you've made. Where have your scores gone up? What improvements do you notice? Which of your STRIVE qualities have become more balanced?

3. *Look for opportunities.* Looking at your third Wheel of Balance, explore which, if any, of your STRIVE qualities were thrown out of balance as a result of the setback. This can help you understand your patterns and devise steps to deal with them.

4. *Make a plan of attack.* As we talked about in this chapter, you overcome setbacks by recommitting to yourself and your goals, so devise a list of action steps you can take to move toward your next stage of development.

YOUR NEXT HORIZON

Cassie

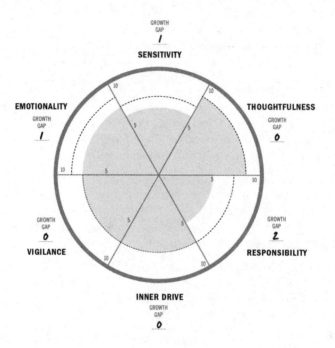

MY NEXT HORIZON IS	
Balancing Responsibility and Inner Drive	
MY ACTIONS ARE	
Getting help from my MIL	Planning a digital detox weekend once per month
Paying for grocery and laundry services	Joining an HR Women in Leadership organization

YOUR *NEXT HORIZON*

_____

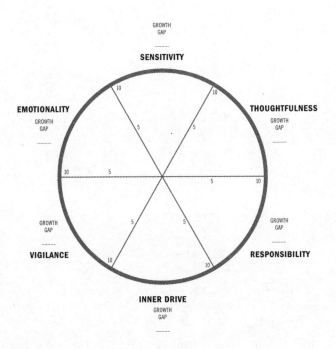

MY NEXT HORIZON IS	
MY ACTIONS ARE	

WHAT'S NEXT?

*"There are always going to be reasons to doubt your
own worth; the question is, how far do you allow
yourself to go down that road before you look up and
realize . . . you had the power to come home all along?"*

—SARA BAREILLES

CONGRATS—YOU DID IT! You have made it to the end of this book. Give yourself a huge pat on the back for all the hard work and effort you have
devoted to this process. You should be very proud of how you have shown
up for yourself every step of the way.

In the Introduction, I expressed the wish that you would stop
doubting yourself, feel in control of your life, and reclaim what success
means to you. I hope that within these pages you found confidence to
turn your sensitive striving into strength and move through the world
with ease.

When I initially had the idea for this book, a handful of publishers
declined it. They didn't believe enough people identified as sensitive, and
that those who did, didn't see it as a positive. But, the more I've talked
about sensitivity, the more I witness our movement growing. Now, I've
spoken to audiences at Stanford, Walmart, and Adweek and continue to
coach managers and leaders at companies like Facebook, IBM, Netflix,
Google, and more. Our community of Sensitive Strivers grows larger
every day. I share this for two reasons. First, to reiterate that you are not

alone, and secondly, to emphasize that it's never been more important for you to stand in your power. As I write this conclusion, we are facing a global recession, record unemployment, and business uncertainty with almost no end in sight. The challenges ahead are enormous, and Sensitive Strivers will be an essential part of leading us through these difficult times. This world is in desperate need of people like you—with innate ingenuity, empathy, and drive to make a positive impact. At the end of the day, your sensitivity and ambition are undeniable gifts, so use them to the fullest.

One reality we can't ignore, though, is that workplaces need to catch up to the value Sensitive Strivers bring to the table. While we've recently seen big shifts toward greater diversity and inclusion, there's a long way to go to appreciate what those with temperamental and neurological differences offer. Companies are only just beginning to realize that Sensitive Strivers are their best and most overlooked assets. Never has it been more important for you to demonstrate all of your attributes and also to claim the recognition and respect you deserve. The time is now to speak up and to be part of a shift to create welcoming workplaces that embrace people with all types of aptitudes in all their glorious differences.

The tools in this book are designed so that you can return to them whenever you need to, in good times and bad, as your goals and seasons of life evolve. After all, trusting yourself isn't a finish line you cross—it's a continuous process. If you didn't get a concept the first time around, revisit it in a week or two. Sometimes it takes a while for a change to sink in. Don't give up on yourself. I also suggest you periodically sit down with the journal you used to catalog your experiences and complete the Exercises in this book. Review your progress and insights to remind yourself how far you have come and all the wisdom you have gained.

Even though this is the end of the book, our journey together doesn't have to end here. Remember to check out the bonus resources for this book, including worksheets, guides, and articles, at melodywilding.com /bonus. There you can also join my free community to connect with thousands of other Sensitive Strivers.

Above all, celebrate yourself for the massive shifts you have created through this book. And thank you so much for allowing me to walk by your side as your guide. Let this last page be the launching pad for the next level of your life and career. You have everything you need. All you need to do now is trust yourself.

ACKNOWLEDGMENTS

WRITING A BOOK IS A THRILLING—AND CHALLENGING—JOURNEY. *Trust Yourself* took over four years to become a reality and I'm incredibly grateful for the community of family, friends, publishing professionals, and colleagues who offered guidance, advice, and a shoulder to lean on along the way.

First, to my other half, Brian. Words can't express how much I adore you. You were my confidant on this endeavor from day one and never hesitated to spend hours helping me flesh out ideas, thoughtfully read and comment on early drafts, or offer moral support. You picked me up and dusted me off when I felt down and doubtful. You have cheered me on and been my biggest champion at every turn. Thank you, and I can't wait to spend our lives together.

To my parents, Nora and Dave, who taught me what it meant to trust myself. You have always encouraged me to march to the beat of my own drum and have been endlessly supportive of me taking an entrepreneurial path. Not only that, but you also gave me the gifts of strength, perseverance, and unconditional love, which I draw on daily. This book is for you, and I hope it makes you proud.

Dianne and Barry, thank you for welcoming me into your family with open arms. You've been so supportive of my career, which has meant everything.

Thank you to my grandmother Harriet as well as Grandpa Vince, and Poppi and Nonni in heaven.

Now, to the team behind the book, starting with my amazing agent, Lisa DiMona, who believed in this book even when it was an unformed seedling of an idea. Thank you for your patience while it bloomed. Your steadfast commitment and insightful counsel has helped me navigate this process smoothly and successfully.

I am indebted to the top-notch team at Chronicle Books and Chronicle Prism, including Cara Bedick, whose editorial skills and savvy elevated this book to the next level. I'm so appreciative for your hard work, collaboration, and frequent inspiration.

I also want to thank Chronicle Prism's managing director, Mark Tauber, who enthusiastically supported this book from the beginning and chose to make it a lead title in Chronicle's lineup. Thanks goes to Jennifer Jensen for her marketing magic and to the Chronicle sales team for getting this book into the world. I am grateful to copyeditor Jamie Real, Cecilia Santini, and Pamela Geismar and the Chronicle design team for their creativity and persistence in finding the "just right" look and feel.

There's no way this book would exist without Julie Mosow, who instantly saw my vision and helped shape the proposal into the manuscript that exists today. I am incredibly grateful for the countless hours you spent discussing concepts and for the sharp storytelling lens and polish you brought to the book. Thank you for being my partner in crime. I am so grateful for our work together. I must also thank Brooke Carey, who patiently helped shape my rough proposal into a standout idea, and Meghan Stevenson for her editorial assistance when this book was in its infancy.

To my mastermind partners, Lee Chaix McDonough and Emily Walker: I deeply cherish your friendship and appreciate all of your feedback and input, especially on the exercises.

As I was writing the book, I was lucky to have a powerhouse team behind me, supporting my coaching business. Thank you Rebekah Rius and Sarah McNeal for freeing up the space I needed to write.

To Dr. Elaine Aron, whose research I draw on throughout the book. Thank you for your decades of work on the science of sensitivity and proving to the world that feeling deeply is nothing to apologize for. Dr. Aron has influenced my thinking in meaningful ways, so if you enjoyed this book, then I encourage you to read her books as well.

Thank you to the many friends and colleagues who checked in on me during the writing process. Your kind words and support were invaluable, especially during the difficult moments that inevitably come with putting complex thoughts to paper.

Thank you to my clients, past and present, who have chosen me to serve as their coach. Your stories and transformations built the basis for this book and the entire concept of sensitive striving. Your resilience and courage astound me and it's an honor to be part of your journeys.

To the members of The Haven and my online community across the world. You inspire me to do this work each and every day. It's a privilege to help you.

And finally, to you, the reader. Thank you for spending your precious time reading this book. I hope it has served you well.

NOTES

1. ARE YOU A SENSITIVE STRIVER?

Page 14: *30 percent of sensitive people are extroverted:* Strickland, J. "Introversion, Extroversion and the Highly Sensitive Person." *The Highly Sensitive Person,* April 24, 2018. https://hsperson.com/introversion-extroversion-and-the-highly-sensitive-person/

Page 16: *lead to sensory-processing sensitivity (SPS):* Aron, E. N., and Aron, A. "Sensory-processing sensitivity and its relation to introversion and emotionality." *Journal of Personality and Social Psychology,* vol. 73, no. 2 (1997). 345–368.

Page 16: *more active mental circuitry and neurochemicals in areas related to attention, action-planning, decision-making, and having strong internal experiences:* Acevedo, B., et al. "The highly sensitive brain: an fMRI study of sensory processing sensitivity and response to others' emotions." *Brain and Behavior,* vol. 4, no. 4 (2014). 580–594. https://www.ncbi.nlm.nih.gov/pmc/articles/PMC4086365/

Page 16: *an "innate survival strategy," which helped sensitive people cope with the unpredictability of prehistoric times:* Aron, E. "Is this you?" Retrieved from https://hsperson.com/ [accessed 01/26/2020]

Page 16: *managers consistently rate people with higher sensitivity as their top contributors:* Ramsay, J. "Highly Sensitive People in the workplace—from shame to fame." HRZone, January 2, 2014. https://www.hrzone.com/perform/people/highly-sensitive-people-in-the-workplace-from-shame-to-fame

Page 17: *a 2015 study published in the* Australian Journal of Psychology *found that high sensitivity is linked to greater feelings of distress because of the way sensitive people internally process emotions:* Brindle, K., et al. "Is the relationship between sensory-processing sensitivity and negative affect mediated by emotional regulation?" *Australian Journal of Psychology,* vol. 67, no. 4 (2015). 214–221. https://doi.org/10.1111/ajpy.12084

Page 18: *While current research suggests there are no gender differences in sensitivity between women and men:* Aron, E. *The Highly Sensitive Person: How to Thrive When the World Overwhelms You* (New York: Broadway Books, 1996). 75.

Page 18: *By their teens, nearly 45 percent of girls say they are not allowed to fail:* Ypulse. "The Confidence Code for Girls," 2018. Retrieved from https://static1.squarespace.com/static/588b93f6bf629a6bec7a3bd2/t/5ac39193562fa73cd8a07a89/1522766258986/The+Confidence+Code+for+Girls+x+Ypulse.pdf [accessed 01/26/2020]

Page 18: *They react to stress with excessive worrying and by personalizing negative situations:* "Teenage Girls Are Exposed to More Stressors That Increase Depression Risk." Association for Psychological Science, October 8, 2014. https://www.psychologicalscience.org/news/releases/teenage-girls-are-exposed-to-more-stressors-that-increase-depression-risk.html

Page 18: *Stereotypical beliefs . . . at the same pace as their male counterparts:* Prentice, D., and Carranza, E. "What Women and Men Should Be, Shouldn't Be, and Don't Have to Be: The Contents of Prescriptive Gender Stereotypes." *Psychology of Women Quarterly*, vol. 26 (2002). 269–281. https://journals.sagepub.com/doi/10.1111/1471-6402.t01-1-00066

Page 18: *Even though studies show that at infancy, newborn boys are more emotionally reactive than girls:* Kraemer, S. "The Fragile Male." *The BMJ*, vol. 321 (2000). 1609–1612. https://www.ncbi.nlm.nih.gov/pmc/articles/PMC1119278/

2. OVERCOME THE HONOR ROLL HANGOVER

Page 36: *one of the biggest problems with overfunctioning:* Lerner, H. *The Dance of Anger: A Woman's Guide to Changing the Patterns of Intimate Relationships* (New York: Harper & Row, 1985). 27.

Page 37: *wrote for* BuzzFeed: Petersen, A. H. "How Millennials Became the Burnout Generation." *BuzzFeed*, January 5, 2019. https://www.buzzfeednews.com/article/annehelenpetersen/millennials-burnout-generation-debt-work

Page 38: *Your brain . . . making other people happy:* Berridge, K. C., and Robinson, T. E. "What is the role of dopamine in reward: hedonic impact, reward learning, or incentive salience?" *Brain Research Reviews*, vol. 28 (1998). 309–369. https://lsa.umich.edu/psych/research&labs/berridge/publications/Berridge&RobinsonBrResRev1998.pdf

Page 38: *can lead to anxiety and depression:* Shensa, A., et al. "Social Media Use and Depression and Anxiety Symptoms: A Cluster Analysis." *American Journal of Health Behavior*, vol. 42 (2019). 116–128. https://www.ncbi.nlm.nih.gov/pmc/articles/PMC5904786/

Page 38: *worse work performance:* Andreassen, C., et al. "Use of online social network sites for personal purposes at work: does it impair self-reported performance?" *Comprehensive Psychology*, vol. 3 (2014). 1–21. https://journals.sagepub.com/doi/full/10.2466/01.21.CP.3.18

Page 38: *studies show that higher-income workers experience more stress:* Petrone, P. "Stress at Work—See Who's Feeling It the Most and How to Overcome It." *The Learning Blog—LinkedIn*, April 17, 2018. https://learning.linkedin.com/blog/working-together/stress-at-work-_-see-whos-feeling-it-the-most

Page 38: *neglect downtime:* U.S. Travel Association. "Time Off and Vacation Usage." Retrieved from https://www.ustravel.org/toolkit/time-and-vacation-usage [accessed 03/13/2020]

3. GIVE YOURSELF PERMISSION

Page 51: *Fran Hauser, media executive and author:* Hauser, F. *The Myth of the Nice Girl: Achieving a Career You Love without Becoming a Person You Hate* (Boston: Houghton Mifflin Harcourt, 2018). 31–32.

Page 54: *I love this trick from Brené Brown:* Brown, B. *Daring Greatly: How the Courage to Be Vulnerable Transforms the Way We Live, Love, Parent, and Lead* (New York: Gotham Books, 2012). 171.

4. CHANNEL EMOTIONS INTO AN ADVANTAGE

Page 65: *sensitive people tend to be more ashamed of their feelings and to believe that there's nothing they can do about them:* Brindle, K., et al. "Is the relationship between sensory-processing sensitivity and negative affect mediated by emotional regulation?" *Australian Journal of Psychology*, vol. 67, no. 4 (2015). 214–221. https://doi.org/10.1111/ajpy.12084

Page 66: *high-intensity emotions can compromise your immune system, memory, and attention span:* Seppälä, E. "Your High-Intensity Feelings May Be Tiring You Out." *Harvard Business Review*, February 1, 2016. https://hbr.org/2016/02/your-high-intensity-feelings-may-be-tiring-you-out

Page 66: *accepting your emotions . . . overall life satisfaction:* Ford, B. Q., et al. "The psychological health benefits of accepting negative emotions and thoughts: Laboratory, diary, and longitudinal evidence." *Journal of Personality and Social Psychology*, vol. 115 (2018): 1075–1092 https://www.ncbi.nlm.nih.gov/pubmed/28703602

Page 67: *90 percent of top performers are also high in emotional intelligence:* TalentSmart. "About Emotional Intelligence." Retrieved from https://www.talentsmart.com/about/emotional-intelligence.php [accessed 03/13/2020]

Page 67: *92 percent of executives rate soft skills:* BetterUp. "Leadership Gap." Retrieved from https://www.betterup.com/en-us/leadership-gap [accessed 03/13/2020]

Page 67: *Teams with emotional leaders have greater trust, perform better, and innovate more:* Duhigg, C. "What Google Learned from Its Quest to Build the Perfect Team." *New York Times*, February 28, 2016. https://www.nytimes.com/2016/02/28/magazine/what-google-learned-from-its-quest-to-build-the-perfect-team.html

Page 67: *75 percent of hiring managers said they would be more likely to promote an employee who is emotionally in touch:* Career Builder. "Seventy-One Percent of Employers Say They Value Emotional Intelligence over IQ, According to CareerBuilder Survey." Retrieved from https://www.careerbuilder.com/share/aboutus/pressreleasesdetail.aspx?id=pr652&sd=8/18/2011&ed=08/18/2011 [accessed 03/13/2020]

Page 67: *Because they are more attuned to their inner workings . . . achievement of long-term goals:* Goleman, D. *Emotional Intelligence: Why It Can Matter More Than IQ* (New York: Bantam Dell, 1995). 43.

Page 67: *Your nervous system is designed to go through regular cycles of charge and discharge, stimulation and relaxation:* Nagoski, A., and Nagoski, E. *Burnout: The Secret to Unlocking the Stress Cycle* (New York: Ballantine Books, 2019). 5–12.

Page 68: *Grounding activates your parasympathetic nervous system:* Gerritsen, R., and Band, G. "Breath of Life: The Respiratory Vagal Stimulation Model of Contemplative Activity." *Frontiers of Human Neuroscience*, vol. 12 (2018). 397. https://www.ncbi.nlm.nih.gov/pmc/articles/PMC6189422/

Page 68: *When your parasympathetic nervous system switches on:* Hölzel, B., et al. "Mindfulness practice leads to increases in regional brain gray matter density." *Psychiatry Research*, vol. 191 (2011). 36–43. https://www.ncbi.nlm.nih.gov/pmc/articles/PMC3004979/

Page 70: *Studies show that naming your emotions immediately releases their grip over you:* Torre, J., and Lieberman, M. "Putting Feelings into Words: Affect Labeling as Implicit Emotion Regulation." *Emotion Review*, vol. 10 (2018). 116–124. https://journals.sagepub.com/doi/full/10.1177/1754073917742706

5. OVERHAUL YOUR OVERTHINKING

Page 81: *research shows certain personality types are more likely to develop mental health issues:* Krueger, R., et al. "Personality Traits Are Differentially Linked to Mental Disorders: A Multitrait-Multidiagnosis Study of an Adolescent Birth Cohort." *Journal of Abnormal Psychology*, vol. 105 (1996): 299–312. http://citeseerx.ist.psu.edu /viewdoc/download?doi=10.1.1.482.8192&rep=rep1&type=pdf

Page 81: *Overthinking is driven by negative self-talk, which in psychology is more well known as cognitive distortions:* Burns, D. *The Feeling Good Handbook.* (New York: Harper Collins, 1989). 7–11.

6. TRUST YOUR GUT

Page 96: *his "pause and check" system, as researcher Elaine Aron calls it:* Aron, E., and Aron, A. "Sensory-processing sensitivity and its relation to introversion and emotionality." *Journal of Personality and Social Psychology*, vol. 73 (1997). 345–368. https://www.ncbi.nlm.nih.gov/pubmed/9248053

Page 97: *intuition works on implicit memory:* Wippich, W. "Intuition in the context of implicit memory." *Psychological Research,* vol. 56 (1994). 104–109. https://link .springer.com/article/10.1007/BF00419717

Page 98: *There's a vast neural network of 100 million neurons lining your entire digestive tract:* Johns Hopkins Medicine. "The Brain-Gut Connection," Retrieved from https://www.hopkinsmedicine.org/health/wellness-and-prevention/the-brain -gut-connection [accessed 03/13/20]

Page 98: *One study found that hedge-fund traders:* Kandasamy, N. "Interoceptive Ability Predicts Survival on a London Trading Floor." *Scientific Reports*, vol. 6 (2016). https://www.nature.com/articles/srep32986

Page 98: *"energetic sensitivity":* HeartMath Institute. "Science of the Heart: Exploring the Role of the Heart in Human Performance." Retrieved from https://www. heartmath.org/research/science-of-the-heart/energetic-communication/ [accessed 03/13/20]

Page 98: *leading to deeper awareness, energy, and composure:* HeartMath Institute. "Research FAQs." Retrieved from https://www.heartmath.org/support/faqs /research/ [accessed 03/13/20]

Page 99: *type of innovation-by-hunch is responsible for world-changing discoveries like penicillin and Velcro:* Orf, D. "10 Awesome Accidental Discoveries." *Popular Mechanics,* June 27, 2013. https://www.popularmechanics.com/science/health /g1216/10-awesome-accidental-discoveries/

Page 99: *what psychologists call the "default network":* Beaty, R., et al. "Robust prediction of individual creative ability from brain functional connectivity." *Proceedings of the National Academy of Sciences of the United States of America*, vol. 115 (2018): 1087–1092. https://www.pnas.org/content/115/5/1087

Page 99: *Intuitive thinking stimulates . . . so that the essential stuff gets through:* Arguinchona, J., and Tadi, P. "Neuroanatomy, Reticular Activating System." In *StatPearls* (Treasure Island, FL: StatPearls Publishing, 2019). https://www.ncbi.nlm.nih.gov/books /NBK549835/

Page 99: *Research shows . . . gives you more confidence in your choices than relying on intellect alone:* Lufityanto, G., et al. "Measuring Intuition: Nonconscious Emotional

Information Boosts Decision Accuracy and Confidence." *Psychological Science*, vol. 27 (2016). 622–634. https://doi.org/10.1177/0956797616629403

Page 99: *That's because relying on rapid cognition, or thin-slicing:* Gladwell, M. *Blink: The Power of Thinking without Thinking* (New York: Little, Brown, and Company, 2005). 33–34.

Page 100: *Liz Fosslien . . . letting your gut lead the way:* Fosslien, L., and Duffy, M. *No Hard Feelings: The Secret Power of Embracing Emotions at Work* (New York: Portfolio, 2019), 79–80.

Page 103: *Studies have shown . . . gut-based decisions are a better reflection of their authentic selves:* Maglio, S., and Reich, T. "Feeling Certain: Gut Choice, the True Self, and Attitude Certainty." *American Psychological Association*, vol. 19 (2019). 876–888. https://www.apa.org/pubs/journals/releases/emo-emo0000490.pdf

Page 104: *You make hundreds of decisions a day:* Wansink, B., and Sobal, J. "Mindless Eating: The 200 Daily Food Decisions We Overlook." *Environment and Behavior*, vol. 39 (2007). 106-123. https://doi.org/10.1177/0013916506295573

7. BUILD BOUNDARIES LIKE A BOSS

Page 115: *Rubin always found it hard to be who she was:* Rubin, G. "The importance of knowing what you LIKE to do, and then doing it." Retrieved from https://gretchenrubin.com/2007/04/the_importance_ [accessed 03/13/20]

Page 115: *her inspiration to "Be Gretchen" originated from a conversation with Justice Sandra Day O'Connor:* Osakwe, A. "'The Happiness Project' author Gretchen Rubin talks secrets to happiness." ABC News, November 15, 2017. https://abcnews.go.com/Business/author-gretchen-rubin-talks-finding-happiness-life/story?id=51149122

Page 121: *Claire Wasserman, founder of Ladies Get Paid:* "Ladies Get Paid: About the Book." Retrieved from https://www.simonandschuster.com/books/Ladies-Get-Paid/Claire-Wasserman/9781797102689 [accessed 4/24/2020]

8. SHOW UP AS YOUR FULL SELF

Page 135: *For three years he created an "Integrity Report":* Clear, J. "My 2016 Integrity Report." Retrieved from https://jamesclear.com/2016-integrity-report [accessed 03/14/2020]

9. AIM YOUR AMBITION

Page 151: *Work by BJ Fogg, Director of the Behavior Design Lab at Stanford University . . . 65 percent of people say that tiny habits ripple out:* Chang, J. "Tiny habits: behavior scientist BJ Fogg explains a painless strategy to personal growth." Success (2015). https://www.questia.com/magazine/1G1-346533128/tiny-habits-behavior-scientist-bj-fogg-explains-a

Page 152: *when you do so your body releases endorphins that reinforce a feeling of competence:* Dfarhud, D., et al. "Happiness & Health: The Biological Factors- Systematic Review Article." *Iran Journal of Public Health*, vol. 43 (2014). 1468–1477. https://www.ncbi.nlm.nih.gov/pmc/articles/PMC4449495/

Page 152: *gratitude has many benefits, from improved health to better sleep and happier moods:* Allen, S. "Is Gratitude Good for Your Health?" Retrieved from https://greatergood.berkeley.edu/article/item/is_gratitude_good_for_your_health

Page 154: *framing a goal as questions increases achievement by 27 to 28 percent:* Wilding, S., et al. "The question-behaviour effect: A theoretical and methodological review and meta-analysis." *European Review of Social Psychology*, vol. 27 (2016). 196–230. https://www.tandfonline.com/doi/full/10.1080/10463283.2016.1245940

Page 154: *Tim Ferriss . . . recommends asking yourself:* Ferriss, T. "Q&A with Tim—On Happiness, Dating, Depressive Episodes, and Much More (#390)." Retrieved from https://tim.blog/2019/10/10/tim-on-happiness-dating-depressive-episodes/ [accessed 03/14/2020]

10. FIND THE RIGHT FIT

Page 163: *According to a study conducted by Elaine Aron and her colleagues:* Jagiellowicz, J., et al. "Relationship between the temperament trait of sensory processing sensitivity and emotional reactivity." *Social Behavior and Personality*, vol. 44 (2016). 185–200. https://doi.org/10.2224/sbp.2016.44.2.185

Page 163: *Studies show . . . you experience your work as more meaningful:* Scroggins, W. "Antecedents and Outcomes of Experienced Meaningful Work: A Person-Job Fit Perspective." *Journal of Business Inquiry* (2008). 68–78. https://pdfs.semanticscholar.org/8da8/ccc6a2e141bd41f6dce42e588911affefd5e.pdf

Page 164: *Fitting your career to your personality . . . translates to better performance on the job:* Sylva, H., et al. "Person-job fit and proactive career behaviour: A dynamic approach." *European Journal of Work and Organizational Psychology*, vol. 28 (2019). 631–645. https://doi.org/10.1080/1359432X.2019.1580309

Page 164: *People with the best fit between their personality and their job earned up to a month's salary:* Denissen, J., et al. "Uncovering the Power of Personality to Shape Income." *Psychological Science*, vol. 29 (2018). 3–13. https://doi.org/10.1177/0956797617724435

Page 164: *A strong person-job fit is also linked to greater engagement, energy, enthusiasm, and innovation at work:* Huang, W., et al. "Person–Job Fit and Innovation Behavior: Roles of Job Involvement and Career Commitment." *Frontiers in Psychology*, vol. 10 (2019). 1134. https://www.ncbi.nlm.nih.gov/pmc/articles/PMC6532537/

Page 164: *more than 87 percent of today's businesses are making inclusion a top priority:* PwC. "Global diversity & inclusion survey." Retrieved from https://www.pwc.com/gx/en/services/people-organisation/global-diversity-and-inclusion-survey.html#data [accessed 04/24/2020]

Page 164: *The trend toward hiring neurodiverse leaders:* Austin, R., and Pisano, G. "Neurodiversity as a Competitive Advantage." *Harvard Business Review*, May/June 2017. https://hbr.org/2017/05/neurodiversity-as-a-competitive-advantage

Page 164: *increasing incivility:* Owens, D. "Incivility Rising." Retrieved from https://www.shrm.org/hr-today/news/hr-magazine/pages/0212owens.aspx [accessed 04/24/20]

Page 171: *Pamela Slim . . . says:* Slim, P. "Body of Work Workbook." Retrieved from https://pamelaslim.com/bow-workbook/ [accessed 04/24/2020]

Page 171: *You can also proactively customize your role to find more career satisfaction:* Wrzesniewski, A., and Dutton, J. "Crafting a Job: Revisioning Employees as Active Crafters of Their Work." *Academy of Management Review*, vol. 26 (2001). 179–201. https://doi.org/10.5465/amr.2001.4378011

11. TAKE SMART RISKS

Page 181: *a survey of senior executives identified:* Sahadi, J. "It usually takes 24 years to become CEO. Here's why Risk Takers get there faster." CNN, October 3, 2019. https://www.cnn.com/2019/10/03/success/risk-takers-to-ceo/index.html

Page 183: *Feelings are not in opposition to logical reasoning; they provide essential support for it:* Vries, M., et al. "Fitting decisions: Mood and intuitive versus deliberative decision strategies." *Cognition and Emotion*, vol. 22 (2008). 931–943. https://doi org/10.1080/02699930701552580

Page 183: *Studies show that people accept risks because they value an activity:* Zinn, J. "The meaning of risk-taking—key concepts and dimensions." *Journal of Risk Research*, vol. 22 (2019). 1–15. https://doi.org/10.1080/13669877.2017.1351465

Page 184: *And tackling low stakes . . . improve focus, determination, and emotional resilience:* McGonigal, J. "Building Resilience by Wasting Time." *Harvard Business Review*, October 2012. https://hbr.org/2012/10/building-resilience-by-wasting-time

Page 185: *exposing yourself to stressful situations can lessen fear and avoidance by up to 90 percent:* Kaplan, J., and Tolin, D. "Exposure Therapy for Anxiety Disorders." *Psychiatric Times*, vol. 29 (2011). 33. https://www.psychiatrictimes.com/anxiety /exposure-therapy-anxiety-disorders

Page 187: *Noah Kagan, founder of product marketing startup SumoMe, advises:* Ferriss, T. *Tools of Titans: The Tactics, Routines, and Habits of Billionaires, Icons, and World-Class Performers* (Boston: Houghton Mifflin Harcourt, 2016). 325.

Page 190: *studies show that overthinking leads to slower decision-making and fewer risks:* Adams, J. "Risk taking and the decision making process." *Project Management Quarterly*, vol. 5 (1974). 20–25. https://www.pmi.org/learning/library/risk-taking -decision-making-process-1971

12. SPEAK UP AND STAND YOUR GROUND

Page 201: *Beyond boosting your self-esteem and helping you avoid burnout:* Mayo Clinic Staff. "Being assertive: Reduce stress, communicate better." Retrieved from https://www.mayoclinic.org/healthy-lifestyle/stress-management/in-depth /assertive/art-20044644 [accessed 04/24/2020]

13. BOUNCE BACK FROM SETBACKS

Page 216: *Not only is this okay; it's normal, because of the phenomenon of the change curve:* Gentry, B. "Coaching people through the Change Curve." Retrieved from https://www.insights.com/media/1086/coaching-people-through-the-change -curve.pdf [accessed 05/30/2020]

Page 224: *it takes five positive interactions to outweigh one negative one:* Benson, K. "The Magic Relationship Ratio, According to Science." Retrieved from https://www .gottman.com/blog/the-magic-relationship-ratio-according-science/

ABOUT THE AUTHOR

MELODY WILDING, LMSW, is the workplace success coach for smart, sensitive high achievers who are tired of getting in their own way. Named one of *Business Insider*'s "Most Innovative Coaches," her executive coaching clients include CEOs, C-level leaders, and managers at top Fortune 500 companies such as Google, HP, Facebook, Twitter, Netflix, Verizon, IBM, J.P. Morgan, Pfizer, and others. Melody's work has been featured in the *New York Times*, *Oprah Magazine*, NBC News, the *Washington Post*, *USA Today*, *TIME*, *New York* magazine, the *Chicago Tribune*, *Fast Company*, and dozens of other national media outlets. Through her coaching programs, talks, and small-group workshops, she's here to help you break free from self-doubt and imposter syndrome, master your emotions, and use your sensitivity as the superpower that it is.

Melody is a licensed social worker with a master's degree from Columbia University, and a former psychology researcher at Rutgers University. She is also a professor of human behavior at Hunter College and is a columnist for magazines such as *Forbes* and *Quartz*. She lives in New Jersey with her fiancé, Brian. Learn more at melodywilding.com.